DIVINE ACCOUNTING

SYNKRISIS

Comparative Approaches to Early Christianity in Greco-Roman Culture

SERIES EDITORS

Dale B. Martin (Yale University) and L. L. Welborn (Fordham University)

Synkrisis is a project that invites scholars of early Christianity and the Greco-Roman world to collaborate toward the goal of rigorous comparison. Each volume in the series provides immersion in an aspect of Greco-Roman culture, so as to make possible a comparison of the controlling logics that emerge from the discourses of Greco-Roman and early Christian writers. In contrast to older "history of religions" approaches, which looked for similarities between religions in order to posit relations of influence and dependency, Synkrisis embraces a fuller conception of the complexities of culture, viewing Greco-Roman religions and early Christianity as members of a comparative class. The differential comparisons promoted by Synkrisis may serve to refine and correct the theoretical and historical models employed by scholars who seek to understand and interpret the Greco-Roman world. With its allusion to the rhetorical exercises of the Greco-Roman world, the series title recognizes that the comparative enterprise is a construction of the scholar's mind and serves the scholar's theoretical interests.

DIVINE ACCOUNTING

Theo-Economics in Early Christianity

JENNIFER A. QUIGLEY

Yale

UNIVERSITY PRESS

New Haven and London

Published with assistance from the foundation established in memory of Amasa Stone Mather of the Class of 1907, Yale College.

Yale University Press books may be purchased in quantity for educational, business, or promotional use. For information, please e-mail sales.press@yale.edu (U.S. office) or sales@yaleup.co.uk (U.K. office).

Set in Janson type by Newgen North America.
Printed in the United States of America.

Library of Congress Control Number: 2020947045
ISBN 978-0-300-25316-0 (hardcover : alk. paper)

A catalogue record for this book is available from the British Library.

This paper meets the requirements of ANSI/NISO Z39.48-1992 (Permanence of Paper).

10 9 8 7 6 5 4 3 2 1

Contents

Acknowledgments

I AM GRATEFUL FOR all who helped shape and support this project. My colleagues at Drew University Theological School are brilliant teachers and scholars, and I am especially appreciative of Kate Ott, who has been an enthusiastic mentor and friend. Dean Javier Viera and Associate Dean Melanie Johnson-DeBaufre have been incredibly supportive of this project. My thanks as well to Hilary Floyd, who has been a meticulous research assistant. The book would not exist in this form without her labor. Drew Ph.D. students Darryl Bloodsaw, Julian Cook, Hilary Floyd, Wren Hillis, Jennifer Maidrand, and Kelsey Wallace participated in my spring 2019 Economy and the Bible seminar and provided brilliant conversation partners and readers of this book in development. I am grateful to the students in my Letters of Paul class, who always ask the most creative and important questions and from whom I learn so much.

The faculty in New Testament and early Christianity at Harvard Divinity School (HDS) have been generous with their time, offered helpful critiques, and inspired me with their own scholarship. My deep thanks to Giovanni Bazzana, Karen King, and Elisabeth Schüssler Fiorenza. I am especially grateful for my advisor, Laura Nasrallah, who is a generous mentor, tireless advocate, and deeply thoughtful teacher, scholar, and reader.

My thanks to the cohort of doctoral students at HDS, who modeled collegiality both during their time in the program and far beyond; to Margaret Butterfield, Jung Choi, Chris Hoklotubbe, Roberto Mata, Tyler Schwaller, and Katherine Shaner, who have come before; to Greg Given, Sarah Griffis, Eunyung Lim, Karen Connor McGugan, Heather McLetchie Leader, and Kelsi Morrison-Atkins, my colleagues in the doctoral dissertation seminar, whose generous reading and wise responses have strengthened this book and whose own brilliant dissertation work influences my own. My thanks to Chance Bonar, Lydia Bremer, Jordan Conley, Sarah Porter, Luan Ribiero, and Jeremy Williams for continuing to grow the scholarly community that we have together. I am indebted especially to Greg Given and Lydia Bremer for their meticulous and careful reading of this text. I am grateful to all for their friendship.

My research, writing, and teaching have been deeply informed by colleagues in the Louisville Institute Postdoctoral Fellowship, including Mary Emily Briehl Duba, Kyle Brooks, Jaisy Joseph, Kyle Lambelet, Jennifer Owens-Jofré Salih Sayilgan, and Mike Walker. Edwin Aponte and the staff of the Louisville Institute have provided not only funding support but also generous mentoring. I am also grateful for my doctoral cohort colleagues from Harvard's Committee on the Study of Religion, with whom I enrolled in REL 2001, including Charisse Barron, Austin Campbell, Gregory Clines, Kyrah Daniels, Janan Delgado, Joanna Greenlee, Filipe Maia, Michael Motia, Axel Takács, Craig Tichelkamp, Lina Verchery, Funlayo Wood, and Kimberly Wortmann.

I have been fortunate to have had several opportunities to research, write, and present work that have shaped the direction of this book. My thanks to the Dumbarton Oaks Byzantine Coins and Seals Summer Program and to Eurydice Georganteli and Jonathan Shea. I am grateful to have had the opportunity to complete a numismatics internship at the Harvard University Art Museums, and I thank Carmen Arnold-Biucchi for her mentorship and supervision. I am grateful to Humboldt Universität zu Berlin and to Cilliers Breytenbach for hosting me in a student exchange. I have received helpful feedback on this project from presentations at the annual and international meetings of the Society of Biblical Literature and the conference "Philippi: From Colonia Augusta to Communitas Christiania: Religion and Society in Transition." Joseph Marchal provided engaged and incisive response as I edited this manuscript. My gratitude to HDS for its travel funding support, including the HDS Conference Fund and the Pfeiffer Fund; I am also indebted to the Marion and Jasper Whiting Foundation Fellowship Travel Grant. I have received generous support for dedicated writing time, and I am grateful to the Woodrow Wilson Foundation for the Charlotte W. Newcombe Doctoral Dissertation Fellowship and to HDS for the Dean's Dissertation Fellowship. I owe many thanks to Kathryn Kunkel, the Th.D. program coordinator, for her generous help throughout my doctoral program.

A word of gratitude to Robert Allan Hill and the many colleagues and friends of the Marsh Chapel community, saints too numerous to name. I am a better scholar and teacher because of students from Boston University from whom I have learned so much: Thomas Batson, Jennifer Bishop, Abigail Clauhs, Matthew Cron, Jaimie Dingus, Oelmis Fermin, Devin Harvin, Bethany Kotlar, Robert Lucchesi, Maritt Novak, Phoebe Oler, Emma Pennisi, Rebekah Phillips, Ian Quillen, Nick Rodriguez, Kate Rogers, Kasey Shultz, Tyler Sit, Denise-Nicole Stone, Courtney Tryon, Demarius Walker, and Savannah Wu. My thanks to Gregory Palmer for the institutional support and freedom to pursue my studies.

My family has accompanied me throughout this journey, and I am especially grateful to my parents for constantly reminding me that I can do it. My first lessons in teaching came from home, and my first experiences in research came from the public library—and I have my parents to thank for both. My extended family has offered an incredible network of support, and I am thankful for my grandmother's bottomless wisdom and hot tea.

My greatest thanks go to Soren Hessler, with whom I have learned the most about partnership.

DIVINE ACCOUNTING

Checkbook featuring a quotation from Phil 4:13 (Photo: Copyright © Karen Mancinelli, 2020)

Introduction

THE FIRST SEMESTER OF my doctoral program marked the height of the Occupy Wall Street movement. Harvard Yard was restricted to persons with Harvard identification cards as students camped out day and night in protest.[1] Harvard Divinity School students deeply involved themselves in the movement by protesting, participating in community decision-making,[2] and offering chaplaincy to the protestors in New York City's Zuccotti Park, in downtown Boston, and in Harvard Yard. These moments sparked in me an intense interest in the ways in which religion and economics overlap in Christianity. From groups like The Simple Way, a neo-monastic organization that pools economic resources,[3] and Christian Healthcare Ministries,[4] in which believers support one another's health-care costs with money and prayer, to the "Christian capitalism" of Gary North's Institute of Christian Economics[5] and prosperity gospel preachers such as Creflo Dollar,[6] contemporary Christians use the Bible in diverse ways to think about economy and theology as intertwined. They read and interpret biblical texts to consider God's role in both the structural and the personal financial systems of God's followers, and they use the Bible to regulate right practices and beliefs around money, giving, savings, banking, wealth, and even retirement investments.

These diverse beliefs, practices, and interpretive strategies sometimes take on material form. A checkbook holder (pictured opposite the first page of this Introduction), produced by Christian Art Gifts, includes a quotation from Philippians 4:13: "I can do everything through Him who gives me strength."[7] This checkbook cover is one in a series of options available from Christian Art Gifts. All the checkbook covers deploy biblical, prayer, and hymn citations in order to make statements about both God and the checkbook's intended use. Options include Luke 1:45, "Blessed is she who believes that the Lord would fulfill His promises to her"; Jeremiah 29:11, "'For I know the plans I have for you,' declares the Lord, 'plans to prosper you and not to harm you, plans to give you hope and a future'"; and Joshua 1:9, "Be strong and courageous. Do not be terrified; do not be discouraged, for the Lord will be with you wherever you go." All of these citations operate within theological and economic logics in which God is present in the transaction that occurs when the owner writes a check.

Yet it is the Philippians 4:13 checkbook cover that is irresistible to me, given that this book focuses on theological and economic logics in the Letter to the Philippians. When the owner writes a check, she envelops that transaction in a biblical quotation. The quotation may assuage the financial sting of making a rent payment or other large transaction that still requires a physical check. This message may also project confidence. The checkbook bearer stakes a claim that is both theological and financial to those who are watching a check being written. The writer is confident in God's presence and strength, even at the seemingly mundane level of a simple financial transaction. The entanglement of theological and economic logics often manifests itself in materiality and in material objects. Objects like this checkbook cover raise questions of whether and how humans understand God as an actor as they participate in their day-to-day economic activities and in physical manifestations of these transactions.

Thinking with Theo-Economics

There is significant evidence that our modern scholarly categories of theology and economics were not so clearly delineated and separated in antiquity. Many texts, documents, and objects instead demonstrate what I call theo-economics,[8] or an intertwined theological and economic logic in which divine and human beings regularly enter into transactions with one another. Imagine, for a moment, no separation between economy and theology, between *theologia* and *oikonomia*, between accounting for god(s) and an accounting of the ordered world. We have significant evidence in antiquity that divine and semidivine beings were understood as having vibrant materiality within the economic sphere and that the gods were understood as economic actors, with whom humans could transact.

When I use the term "theo-economics" to describe an ancient context in which divine and human beings regularly transact with one another, I am attempting to capture a complexity about the ancient world that has been difficult for contemporary scholarly disciplines to describe. Bruno Latour described a similar difficulty in exploring the entanglement of science, technology, and society. In *We Have Never Been Modern*, he shares the experience of studying "strange situations that the intellectual culture in which we live does not know how to categorize." While Latour and his colleagues were located in disparate disciplines in the academy, they found themselves "always attempting to retie the Gordian knot by crisscrossing . . . the divide that separates exact knowledge and the exercise of culture. . . . Hybrids ourselves . . . we rely on the notion of translation, or network."[9] Translating an ancient context into an academic conversation, which often siloes the study of the economy from the study of religion in antiquity,[10] requires a word that can retie two areas, theology and economy, that are often treated separately in the contemporary academy.

As Latour ends his book with the image of the Parliament of Things, he acknowledges that "there are times when new words are needed to convene a new assembly."[11] To explore the entangled networks of theology and economics requires assembling together perhaps disparate pieces of evidence. Sometimes, I use theo-economics to describe the ways in which theological thinking is found in spaces, objects, and texts of the activities of the ancient economy, leaning into the ways in which the theological imaginary is lively in mundane economic activities such as banking, storage, purchases, and contracts. Sometimes, I use theo-economics to describe the deployment of explicitly financial language to make theological arguments, leaning into the ways in which the technical language of the economy informs theologies of early Christ communities. Sometimes, I use theo-economics to describe the ways in which multivalent language can have both theological and economic possibilities, leaning into the flexible in-between of the hyphen in theo-economics. Only by assembling these evidentiary networks together can we begin to describe with greater detail both ancient theology and the ancient economy. Throughout, I am using theo-economics as a methodological intervention that keeps to the fore the transactional entanglements of humans and divines and the possibility of divines as economically actant when we read early Christian texts.

My use of "actant" is informed by the work of new materialists, especially Jane Bennett, who have drawn inspiration from Latour's image of the Parliament of Things and who have helped us to understand the interconnectedness of people and the objects around them, to get at the "vital materiality" of nonhuman things such as power grids and garbage dumps—and, I would I would add, economic forces such as "the market." Is it possible to take what Bennett calls "a careful course of anthropomorphization" as a historical methodology?[12] How can a framework toward new materialism, and in particular Bennett's notion of vibrant materiality, help us to ask different questions of early Christian texts, especially the Letter to the Philippians? If "agentic capacity is now seen as differentially distributed across a wider range of ontological types,"[13] we might be able to consider the broader ontological range of antiquity and to include the gods as actant. In doing so, I am describing the ways in which the gods could be both effectual in the ancient economy and affectual for persons transacting with them.

The vibrant materiality of the gods in the ancient economy is why the theo-economic language and imagery found in these texts and objects cannot simply be described as "metaphor."[14] When a goddess has her own bank account, when a god stands to lose his property unless an emperor intervenes, and when divine and semidivine beings receive dedicatory tithes, enter into loan agreements, and create and regulate their own currency, modern scholars need a different framework than "metaphor" to account for these phenomena. Such a framework must take seriously the ancient worldview that divine activity in the economy is not only possible but quite normal.

When we turn to theo-economic language in New Testament and early Christian texts, then, we need to understand such language in its broader historical context. These texts emerge in a context in which we find divine activity in human economics, a divine economy with its own commodities and transactions, and the ability of humans to effect activity within that divine economy. Paul's Letter to the Philippians contains texts such as "For me, living is Christ and dying is gain" (1:21), "I calculate all things as a loss . . . so that I might gain the profit Christ" (3:8), and "And my God will fulfill all your lack according to his riches in Christ Jesus" (4:19). Thinking about these texts with theo-economics opens up the possibility of understanding ordinary divine-human logics that would have been legible to early Christ followers. These earliest Christ followers experienced divine involvement among others, both outside and within their own community.

Another Poverty in Pauline Studies

Pauline studies has changed dramatically since Steven J. Friesen's article "Poverty in Pauline Studies" appeared in 2004. He noted that "poverty is rarely discussed in the study of Paul's assemblies."[15] Poverty is now a significant topic in the field of biblical studies, especially within Pauline studies. Scholars continue to pursue ways to better model the socioeconomic makeup of early Christ-following communities, given the 90 percent or more of persons living near or below subsistence level in antiquity.[16] They have asked a variety of new questions about economic issues and the letters of Paul, which have built on these early questions.[17] There has also emerged an increasing interest in Paul and the financial relationships he maintained with the communities to which he wrote as well as the networked relationships within and among the *ekklēsiai*. This interest has coalesced around two trends: whether Paul accepted financial support from the communities to which he wrote[18] and whether the Pauline corpus contains an ethic of concern for the poor.[19] While these trends intertwine over issues such as the circumstances of

Pauline timeline and biography, they also reflect broader anxieties in the field of New Testament studies over consistency across
the diverse corpus of letters to particular communities in particular
situations.

This first trend, that of Paul's acceptance of financial support,
has driven much of the scholarship on the financial language of the
Letter to the Philippians. Scholars have been, on the one hand, concerned with the idea that Paul would rely on an *ekklēsia* for financial support and, on the other, troubled by conflicting evidence that
suggests that Paul accepts financial support from one community
while claiming financial independence from another community. In
Phil 4:15–19, Paul seems to be offering thanks for financial support
he has received, while in 1 Cor 9:15–18, Paul claims to preach the
gospel free of charge.[20] The picture is complicated by the ways in
which Acts of the Apostles portrays Paul as an independent worker
in conflict with some of the evidence from his letters.[21]

Some scholars, such as J. P. Sampley, have argued that this conflicting evidence among passages about financial support for the *ekklēsiai* demonstrates that Paul has an inconsistent financial policy for
funding his travels and work for the gospel.[22] Other scholars, who
want to see Acts as a reliable source of information about the historical Paul, see Philippians as a bit of an outlier, an exception of Pauline
financial dependence amid a general practice of self-sufficiency.[23]
Still others try to smooth out these inconsistencies by arguing for a
comprehensive financial policy.[24]

The issue of Pauline financial in/dependence matters to scholars who seek to craft a Pauline biography. C. H. Dodd, to take one
example, called Paul a man "not born to a 'proletarian status'" because a "man born to manual labor does not speak self-consciously
of 'labouring with my own hands.'"[25] On Phil 4:15–19, Dodd writes,
"Here Paul is trying to say a graceful word of thanks for a gift of
money. How much he hated taking it, we may infer from 1 Cor
9:15–18. He can scarcely bring himself to acknowledge that the
money was welcome to him, and covers up his embarrassment by
piling up technical terms of trade, as if to give the transaction a
severely 'business' aspect."[26] Dodd's assertion relies heavily on Acts:
Paul is portrayed as a Roman citizen (Acts 22:22–39), with his own
income source as a tentmaker (18:3). Scholars who have followed

in this vein have read the model of Paul's independent work in a variety of ways, whether in light of early rabbinic commitments to a combination of Torah study with working a trade[27] or on the model of traveling Greco-Roman Socratic-Cynic philosophers.[28]

This range of scholarship prioritizes 1 Cor 9:15–18, in which Paul preaches the gospel free of charge (*adapanon*) while earning the reward (*misthos*) of not using up his authority in the gospel. Thus, Paul's "stated missionary policy and practice [is] to be fiscally independent."[29] Yet 1 Cor 9:15–18 is often prioritized over Phil 4:15–19 with little explanation.

Not only do scholars craft a biography of Paul as an industrious worker, but sometimes they also engage in a psychologizing of Paul. Hence Dodd suggests that Paul covers up his "embarrassment" with business terminology. Such an assessment presumes that business terminology is value-neutral. Yet, as this project will show, the deployment of business terminology in the letter, particularly to describe human-divine relationships, is anything but value-neutral. By only focusing on questions of Paul's compensation for the gospel, scholars have missed the opportunity to ask larger questions about human-divine theo-economics, such as the following: Who controls access to the gods? Can the property of the gods, or even the gods themselves, be bought and sold? Who determines the cost to participate in divine-human exchange, and who has the ability to pay that cost? What commodities and persons are valued and devalued in divine-human transactions?

A second trend in recent Pauline studies assesses whether the letters provide evidence for an ethic of concern for the poor. Given the rampant poverty within and around the earliest Christ communities, did Christ followers implement systems of charity and care for the poor among them? And, relatedly, does Paul express in his letters a theology that encompasses care for the poor?

Assumptions about Pauline biography and the relationship between the Pauline corpus and Acts also affect how scholars approach these questions about poverty. Does the Jerusalem collection described in Acts 11 match with the brief and varied references to the financial support Paul seems to solicit and collect from the communities with whom he corresponds, particularly in Galatians 2, Romans 15, and 2 Corinthians 8 and 9? This chapter from Acts, which includes the first reference to the disciples being called "Christians" (11:26), includes a prophecy of a famine reaching Antioch and the agreement of the disciples to send support to brothers and sisters living in Judea. These gifts are mediated through "Barnabas and Saul" (11:30).

When we look at Paul's own (co)writings, we find a slightly different picture. When Paul recounts his détente with other apostles in Jerusalem over bringing the gospel to Gentiles, he argues that he and Barnabas have entered a *koinōnia*,[30] a partnership arrangement, with the other apostles and that they exhorted him to remember the poor (Gal 2:10). In Rom 15:26, Paul notes that people in Macedonia and Achaia joined in a *koinōnia* for the poor among the saints in Jerusalem.[31] In 2 Corinthians 8 and 9, Paul exhorts the Corinthian assemblies to follow the example they have from the Macedonian assemblies, who give abundantly despite their deep poverty (2 Cor 8:2). How scholars read and understand the historical context of the Letter to the Philippians, especially Philippians 4, depends in no small part on how these texts in Acts and other Pauline letters are interpreted.

Galatians 2, Romans 15, and 2 Corinthians 8 and 9 have formed the backdrop for most recent scholarly debates related to poverty and Pauline studies. Do these short passages provide enough evidence for a formal social program wherein some Christ assemblies took up regular collection for distribution to poorer Christ assemblies? And can these texts demonstrate any sort of "Pauline theology" related to care for the poor? Does Paul want Christ followers to care about the poor, or do his eschatological interests make response to poverty a moot point, in light of a belief in the imminent return of Christ? Bruce W. Longenecker has recently criticized scholars who claim that the Jerusalem collection is a practical concern and that Pauline theology does not address poverty directly.[32] Longenecker instead contends that the poor are a key component to Pauline theology in Christ-following communities and that Paul's agreement to "remember the poor" is integral to the larger theological interests in Galatians and more broadly.[33] Longenecker is correct to critique a separation of response to poverty as a "practical" rather than theological concern, but Longenecker's own work reflects a broader trend within Pauline studies that has solely focused on pov-

erty to the detriment of a fuller understanding of the broad range
of theo-economics in these letters, which were exchanged among
Christ followers who themselves were often poor.

The difficulty with mapping poverty is that it misses the full
range of ways in which theo-economic language is deployed
throughout the Pauline corpus. Care for the poor reflects one aspect of human-human financial relationships. Yet a focus on questions such as the Jerusalem collection and Paul's response to poverty
misses the variety of ways in which Paul deploys financial language
in theological discussions of suffering, resurrection, righteousness,
the gospel, and even Christ, to take a few examples from Philippians.
In a historical context in which persons did not separate the theological from the economic and regularly transacted with the divine,
the scholarly focus on these few verses about poverty is myopic. This
is not to say that poverty is unimportant either to Paul or to Pauline
scholarship. Indeed, it is ethically urgent, as Christian communities
respond to poverty and economic inequality today.[34] Rather, this is
to say that there is a rich variety of theo-economic language in and
among these early Christ-following communities.[35]

When we focus on the poor as objects of charitable concern, and
thus of scholarly study, we miss opportunities to understand the texts
and practices emerging from these poor communities. The poor in
Philippi evidently described abundance even in the face of poverty.
Those who live around subsistence level should not be solely defined in scholarship by their poverty, and neither should their theology be solely read alongside their socioeconomic status. These
early Christ followers imagine the possibilities of transformation—
socially, theologically, and economically—through the gospel in a
variety of ways.

Despite scholarly debate about how poor the early Christ followers were, the communities with which Paul corresponded clearly
included poor persons. Scholars will better understand poverty in
the Pauline correspondence if we not only recognize this poverty in
antiquity but also take seriously the abundant language of gain, loss,
profits, abundance, security, prosperity, and venture that is found
throughout the Letter to the Philippians and the letters ascribed to
Paul. The poverty in Pauline studies over the past twenty years has
been the way in which, by focusing almost exclusively on economic

scales, the details of the Jerusalem collection, and concerns over Pauline ethic for the poor, we have missed the intertwined theological and economic rhetoric that pervades the Pauline corpus. We have therefore failed to see how Paul and other early Christ followers work within but also rework a system in which God is someone who transacts with humans, even poor ones.

Paul and Gift Exchange

Pauline scholarship has also spilled significant ink exploring the language of gift, *charis*, in the letters of Paul. While some of these recent studies are imbricated with the conversations around poverty, Pauline compensation, and collections mentioned earlier,[36] others have tried to focus on a comprehensive analysis of *charis* in the letters of Paul. This trend has emerged from a broader interest in sociology and anthropology about the phenomenon of gift exchange as well as the long afterlife of the language of gifts in the letters of Paul. Christian and especially Protestant theology has emphasized the importance of the term *charis*, frequently translated as "grace," as central to human salvation through divine *charis*. This is due in no small part to the frequent use of the term in Romans and the importance of that letter in Protestant exegesis, especially Martin Luther's commentary on the letter.[37]

James R. Harrison offers an early example of this recent trend, arguing that the broader Greco-Roman system of benefaction helps to explain Paul's understanding of divine and human *charis*. Using a variety of material and literary evidence, Harrison contends that "the familiarity of *charis* and its associated reciprocity conventions ensured its ready recognition by Paul's first-century auditors and would probably have captured their attention as the apostle began to invest the word with new theological content." According to Harrison, Paul uses the motif of the impoverished benefactor to make use of conventions of reciprocity while simultaneously transforming it, allocating the honor that had gone to the wealthy toward "God as the cosmic benefactor and to the socially marginalised in the body of Christ."[38] Harrison's treatment acknowledges the theological and social overlap of *charis* in the letters of Paul, although his description of Paul investing new "theological" content partially occludes the ways in which the broader Greco-Roman system of benefaction already was both theological and financial. Divine-human benefaction, including humans offering benefactions on behalf of devotion to a deity, was a ubiquitous part of the larger theo-economic system of reciprocity.

More recently, John G. M. Barclay's *Paul and the Gift* reconstructs a Pauline theology of "grace" (*charis*) by reconsidering it within the anthropology and history of gift. His project focuses on literary comparanda, especially Jewish construals of divine beneficence in the Second Temple period, in order to contextualize a reading of the Christ-event as a divine gift in Galatians and Romans.[39] Barclay also describes the reception history of Paul on *charis*, with significant focus on Luther's and Calvin's theological interpretations of grace in their readings of Paul.[40] This reception history is both a strength of Barclay's study and also an acknowledgment of the inherent problem of such a study. Long-standing Christian debates emerge around theological concepts such as justification and sanctification that are only reified post-Paul using interpretations of the letters of Paul. These theological concerns drive a scholarly myopia on the language of gift over a rich variety of theo-economic language found throughout the letters of Paul. It is also worth noting that Barclay does not engage with material evidence, whether from inscriptions or papyri, with the exception of four inscriptions filtered through Harrison's earlier study.[41] This skews the available evidence toward the elite and toward the literary and contributes to a de-economizing of gift language in favor of a theological reading. The two are not mutually exclusive.

Thomas R. Blanton's *A Spiritual Economy: Gift Exchange in the Letters of Paul of Tarsus* combines a strong theoretical grounding in the multidisciplinary work in gift exchange, including Jacques Derrida, Marcel Mauss, Pierre Bourdieu, and others, with an engagment with the language of gift exchange throughout the letters of Paul.[42] Blanton's self-stated aims are "(1) to delineate the characteristics of the 'economy' of gift exchange evident in the letters of the first-century Jewish evangelist Paul of Tarsus; and (2) to make use of Paul's letters as a heuristic device through which to clarify and elaborate issues not yet raised in previous studies of gift exchange."[43] Blanton compares the language of gift exchange in Paul with contemporaneous literary texts from Seneca the Younger, Pliny the Elder, and others, focusing more on Greco-Roman than Jewish authors. Blanton offers the most theoretically engaged of the recent studies; by situating this language from Paul's letters in broader studies of gift exchange, he reminds us that "free gifts" are never actually free but rather a part of complex social systems that involve reciprocity and response. Blanton's study also helps to situate the letters of Paul as a source text for cross-cultural anthropological studies of gift exchange. Blanton, like Barclay, engages only with literary evidence, although unlike Barclay, Blanton avoids de-economizing gift language. Multidisciplinary engagement helps Blanton to map the material consequences of symbolic gift exchanges that Paul mediates between God and early Christ communities. Again, though, Blanton relies heavily on Seneca's *De Beneficiis*, which he acknowledges is a difficulty when the senders and recipients of the letters of Paul were not among the elite.

The proliferation of these recent studies[44] represents the ways in which Protestantizing trends in biblical studies continue to influence the questions and topics that are brought to the study of early Christian texts. All of these studies, which in their analyses of the language of gift in the letters of Paul acknowledge the presence of divine-human transactions, stop short of a more expansive view of the possibilities that emerge from the much greater variety of theo-economic language found in the letters of Paul. How does the language of profit, loss, venture, abundance, and lack function alongside the language of *charis*, or gift?

Chapter Outline

One especially fruitful text for consideration of the theme of theo-economics is Paul's Letter to the Philippians.[45] This book explores theo-economics in the language and rhetoric of Philippians, focusing especially on passages in which God or Christ is engaged in transactions among Paul and the Philippians. In addition, I trace one direction of the early Christian exegetical afterlife of the letter's theo-economic themes.

To help reorient our thinking toward seeing theo-economic language in New Testament and early Christian texts, I first explore some of the contexts in which the gods and humans transacted in antiquity. Chapter 1, "Theo-Economics in Antiquity," introduces these contexts through objects: inscriptions, documents, coins, and other material evidence. First, I describe some theo-economic contexts that cultic sites provide, including banking, storage, and land management. From job contracts for religious professionals to imperially mediated disputes over sacred property, gods and humans regularly interacted with one another through the financial systems of temples.[46] Second, I consider examples of non-temple-related transactions. These material comparanda lay the groundwork for the analysis of Philippians throughout the rest of the book. While it would take a book-length project to fully describe the variety of theo-economic possibilities in antiquity, this chapter demonstrates the ubiquity of divine-human transactions and offers a preliminary map of the multiple ways in which theology and economy overlapped.

Chapter 2, "The Venture of the Gospel," considers the theo-economics of Philippians 1, with some consideration of Philippians 4. I focus on the financial valences of *koinōnia*, a term that is often translated as "sharing" or "fellowship" but whose ancient context largely deploys the term in contracts, including land leases and marriage contracts. I consider some of these legal and financial materials, which help demonstrate how *koinōnia* discourse is functioning in the letter. While in a letter like 1 Corinthians we find, as Anna Miller has shown, *ekklēsia* discourse, in Philippians we instead find *koinōnia*. That is, 1 Corinthians uses a political term to describe the organizational relationships among the members of the community, while Philippians uses a theo-economic term to describe the organizational relationship between Paul and the Philippians.[47] By thinking about the broader context of the term as one in which parties share risk and reward, we can better understand how a "*koinōnia* in the gospel*" may have been heard and received as a venture. A focus on the "venture of the gospel" in Phil 1:5 also helps explain the language found in Paul's discussion of his imprisonment as a contribution to the *prokopē* (progress) of the gospel venture (1:12). Thus, even Paul's statement that "living is Christ and dying is gain" in Phil 1:21 has an underlying theo-economic logic. I conclude with an examination of Philippians 4, arguing that it is only within the full theo-economic picture of Philippians 1 that we can understand Philippians 4's language of abundance and lack in relation to the Philippians' financial support for Paul.

In chapter 3, "The Christ Commodity," I turn to Philippians 2–3, focusing on the language of gain and loss in Phil 3:7–11. In this passage, Paul offers a divine-human accounting sheet in which his statuses are counted as losses so that he might gain the profit Christ (Phil 3:8:). I contextualize this passage by reading Lucian's *Lives for Sale*, a text in which gods and humans participate in a human-divine slave market. That is, persons in antiquity sometimes considered the gods to be the source of their financial profits and losses, and sometimes they understood the gods to be dependent on humanity for divine gains and losses. Most importantly, persons in antiquity sometimes discussed the gods as commodities that could be bought, sold, or traded. I then map where the complex theo-economic logics at work in Phil 3:7–11 fit within a variety of literary sources that use similar language of profit and loss to imagine human-divine interdependence. Paul places this commodification of Christ alongside a claim to be in a *koinōnia* of suffering with Christ in order to attain resurrection from the dead. I argue that the commodification of Christ in Philippians 3 makes sense within the larger rhetoric of the letter, especially Phil 2:7, in which Christ is described in slave form. Paul sets up a commodities exchange in which suffering gives him the proper status currency to acquire Christ. The Letter to the Philippians thus represents an early data point in what will emerge as a divine-human economy of suffering in early Christianity.

Chapter 4, "The Down Payment of Righteousness," focuses on a later, related text, Polycarp's *Letter to the Philippians* (Pol. *Phil.*). The letter's seemingly disjointed themes—from its emphasis on the Philippian community as recipients of Pauline correspondence to its focus on quoting the Pastoral Epistles in condemning *philarguria* (love of money) to its intense interest in right belief and practice to its stark imagery of divine judgment—make sense when taken in a broader theo-economic context. I focus especially on Pol. *Phil.* 8.1–2, in which Polycarp introduces the idea that Christ is the "down payment for our righteousness" as a way to understand the interconnected theo-economic themes in this juridically focused letter.

In my conclusion, I return to the Letter to the Philippians, considering the ways in which a framework of theo-economics helps us to better understand the letter. Theo-economics highlights the multiple transactional entanglements of human and divine beings in early Christ communities in Philippi. I also consider some of the broader implications of my approach for New Testament and early Christian studies, for Roman historians, and for the study of religion. By taking seriously the ways in which persons in antiquity understood themselves to be participating in transactions with the divine, we can begin to break down some of the scholarly categories that separate theology from economics.

CHAPTER ONE

Theo-Economics in Antiquity

Mercurio
Aug(usto). sacr(um).
Sex(tus). Satrius. C(aii). f(ilius).
Vol(tinia). Pudens.
[aed(ilis)][.] Philipp(is).
[ex mensu]ris. ini-
[quis aeris p(ondo)] [. . .]

Consecrated to Mercury Augustus.
Sextus Satrius Pudens, son of Caius,
of the tribe Voltinia,
aedile (?) for the Philippians,
(erected this altar) out of false measures for the bronze weights.

—LATIN INSCRIPTION AT PHILIPPI

Roman Economic History and Theo-Economics

IN ANTIQUITY, PEOPLE TOOK seriously the possibility of entering into financial relationships with the divine. One could draw a loan from or lend to a god. Gods and goddesses owned property, held bank accounts, and participated in financial transactions through the mediation of religious and civic officials.[1] From fifth-century BCE *stelai* on the Athenian acropolis recording the annual reports of the *epistatai*, who managed the finances and properties of the city sanctuaries,[2] to the design and minting of Roman imperial coins under Septimius Severus in the early third century CE,[3] over wide geographic and chronological periods the gods are found in nearly every area of the economic sphere in antiquity. In the midst of these divine-human financial transactions, persons with cultural, political, and economic authority often described themselves as intercessors and regulators of these transactions, and the divine was an active participant in what we call the economic sphere.

Classicists have engaged extensively with these objects in order to glean information about the size and structure of the economy and the political networks of antiquity. Yet they have not approached these materials with a religious studies framework that would allow them to explore fully the interactions between gods and humans in antiquity. To take a single example, Beate Dignas's *Economy of the Sacred in Hellenistic and Roman Asia Minor* makes an excellent case for the complex relationships among city, cult, and ruler in Asia Minor.[4] She engages with a wide variety of epigraphic evidence to explore these networks, but she does not fully account for the role of piety in divine-human transactions. Dignas tries, for instance, to explore the phenomenon in Caria of landowners selling property to sacred temples, often to lease back that same land from the god. In considering the way that classicists and archaeologists have tried to account for this phenomenon, she dismisses the long-held theory that these transactions protected the landowners from piracy by making the gods liable. There is no evidence that Mylasa and its neighbors underwent an economic downturn that necessitated such sales.[5] There is no rational-choice economics model that can explain why wealthy landowners sell their land to the gods, even if there is motivation to lease land from temples at low interest rates. Calling "piety and atavism" unsatisfactory, Dignas lands on a theory that encompasses some sort of governmentally endorsed alimentary scheme.[6] But why not take seriously evidence that ancient residents of Mylasa entered into contracts with the gods and were willing to buy and sell lands to them? A transaction may not make good financial sense, but it may make good theo-economic sense. In addition, these inscriptions often record the names of individuals who are responsible for regulating the leases and management of the sacred land. This divine-human bureaucracy allows humans to receive the tangible and intangible benefits of managing and enforcing the boundaries of sacred property.

The role of the gods and religious institutions in the ancient economy has not been a focus in Roman economic history, which has largely centered on questions of macroeconomics. The study of the ancient economy has undergone dramatic shifts in the past twenty-five years, with significant new scholarship and an important comprehensive volume in *The Cambridge Economic History of the Greco-Roman World*.[7] Many of the debates in the field have focused on structural questions, including the form of the ancient economy, whether it conforms, as Moses Finley argues, to a "primitive" model or whether it more closely resembles, as Peter Temin contends, a "market economy."[8] Other popular topics have included demographics,[9] the role of slavery in the ancient economy,[10] and how to use limited evidence to measure indicators of the ancient economy.[11] These topics, which have largely been pursued by economic historians, are also of interest to scholars in New Testament and early Christian studies.

One increasingly influential model has been New Institutional Economics (NIE), developed by Douglass North, which focuses on structure and performance over time.[12] For North and proponents of NIE, "structure" opens up multiple institutions, technologies, and ideologies to study; structure has been of increasing interest to scholars studying early Christianity.[13] NIE potentially offers a way for scholars to make arguments about the ancient economy using evidence from, for example, Greco-Roman associations.[14] Whereas mainstream economics has tended to become more abstract over time, with more concern for theory than for what happens in the real world, proponents of NIE are interested not in how supply and demand determine prices, for example, but with "the factors that determine what goods and services are traded on markets and therefore are priced."[15] In this way, NIE is interested in including the study of why institutions emerge the way that they do. However, this emerging interest has not yet fully engaged with religious institutions or the influence of theological concerns on the structure of the ancient economy. Even NIE, then, for all its promise, has not yet found a way to account for the gods and the way their activity was understood in the ancient economy.

I am interested in how we can begin to develop a model of an ancient theo-economy in which gods and humans both play an active role. To help reorient our thinking toward seeing theo-economic language in the New Testament and early Christian texts, I first explore some of the contexts in which the gods and humans transacted in antiquity. To create an explanatory model, I introduce these contexts through objects: inscriptions, documents, coins, and other material evidence that record some of the varieties of modes in which gods transacted with humans. I organize these examples into two settings: first, I describe some theo-economic contexts that temples provide, including banking, storage, and land management, and second, I consider examples of non-temple-related transactions.

Sacred Storage and Divine Contracts: Theo-Economics at Greco-Roman Cultic Sites

Gods and goddesses often owned significant property. These properties ranged from sacred lands, which could be cultivated or leased for cultivation,[16] to votive offerings, to the income and costs associated with the oversight of sacrificial cult, which required management and oversight.[17] Temples also served as banking and storage centers in antiquity and offered loans.[18] Networks of cultic officials mediated the complex bureaucratic systems involved in running the cult, including overseeing the inventory and managing sacred property.[19] Three examples demonstrate the complexity of officials mediating temple business. The first two examples are inscriptions that come from the Asklepieion on Kos. A late second- or early first-century BCE inscription is carved on the back of an opisthographic, or double-sided, stele of white marble (60 × 49 × 9 cm). The front originally contained an ornamental kymation decoration that was chiseled down for the stone's reuse in the first century CE as a dedicatory inscription in the Asklepieion.[20] The earlier inscription details the responsibilities of the *prostatai*, or appointees, for the annual distribution of the contents of temple storage for Aphrodite Pontia:

τᾶν δὲ κλαικῶν τῶν θησαυρῶν κυριευόντω τοὶ προστάται
καὶ ἀνοιγόντω μετὰ τᾶς ἱερείας, καθ᾽ ἕκαστον ἐνιαυτὸν ἐμ
μηνὶ Δα-

λίωι καὶ τὸ μὲν ἥμισσον ἔστω τᾶς ἱερείας, τὸ δὲ ἥμισσον
ἀναπεμπόν-
τω ἐπὶ τὰν δαμοσίαν τράπεζαν ἐς τὸν ὑφεστακότα τᾶς θεοῦ
λόγον
καὶ λόγον χρηματιζόντω ἐς τὰ δαμόσια γράμματα. τὸ δὲ
χρῆμα τοῦ-
το ὑπαρχέτω ἐς κατασκευάσματα ἃ κα δόξῃ τᾶι ἐκκλησίᾳ καὶ ἐς
ἐπισκευὰν τοῦ ἱεροῦ.

The *prostatai* shall be in charge of the keys of the *thesauroi*
and open them together with the priestess each year in the
month Dalios. Half (of the sum) belongs to the priestess, the
other half they shall send to the public bank where it is put
into the account which the goddess has, and they shall record the transaction in the public archive. This money shall
be available for construction work as the *ekklēsia* decides and
for repair of the sanctuary.[21]

From this inscription, we learn several important things about the
workings of temple economies. The sanctuary owns and manages
secured *thesauroi* (storage containers), for which there is an annual
inventory and distribution, overseen by the *prostatai* and the priestess for Aphrodite Pontia. The goddess Aphrodite Pontia has her
own bank account. This is not unusual. Throughout Greece and
Asia Minor, there are at least twenty-five examples of temples serving as both clients and proprietors of banks. This evidence has a
wide chronology, ranging from the sixth century BCE (Samos) to
the second century CE (Ephesos), and a wide geographical disper-
sion, including temples in Athens, Thebes, Delphi, Delos, Samos,
Kos, Ephesos, Priene, Sardis, and Halicarnassus.[22]

In the case of the preceding inscription, Aphrodite also shares
half of the goods in the *thesauroi* with the priestess in an example
of human-divine profit sharing; the priestess's income is sourced
from this annual inventory. Perhaps most importantly, the inscription describes the role of individuals and communities functioning
as intermediaries and agents of divine business in the world. While
the priestess and *prostatai* manage the financial bureaucracy that includes inventory and divine banking, the goddess also has decisions
about her property decided by an *ekklēsia;* this business includes

maintenance and construction on sacred property. Religious functionaries' job descriptions involve the proper financial management of divine property, but groups also make decisions about and manage divine property in the world.

The second example from Kos dates to the first century BCE. This inscription comes from a white marble stele, broken into four pieces and reused in a doorway in the Asklepieion. The portion on which this part of the inscription is written measures 64 × 40 × 14 cm. There is not enough information on the inscription to determine which deity is referenced in the contract.[23]

[...][τᾶν δὲ κλαικ]ῶιν μίαν μὲν
[ἐχέτ]ωι ὁ ἱερεύ[ς, τὰν δὲ τοὶ προστάται, τὰν δὲ τοὶ τρα]πε[ζ]-
εῖται τᾶς τοῦ θε[οῦ]
[τραπ]έζας. ἀνο[ιγόντωι δὲ ἐμ μηνὶ ?Πεταγειτνύωι] καθ᾽ ἕκαστον
ἐνιαυτὸν [καὶ]
[ἐξ]αιρεύντωι τ[ὸ εὑρεθὲν καὶ ἓν μέρος ἀποδιδόντωι τῶι ἱερ]-
εῖ, τὰ δὲ δ΄θο μέρηι
[φ]ερόντωι ἐπὶ τὰ[ν τράπεζαν ὅπως δοθῆι ἀνάθεμα ἐς το ἱερ]-
όν ἀπὸ τᾶν ἀπαρχᾶν
ἅ κα δόξῃ{ι} τῶι δ[άμωι.][...]

[The *thesauros* should have three keys,] the priest should
    have one [of
the keys, the *prostatai* the second, and] the managers of the
    god's bank
the third. They should open [it in the month of Petageitn-
    yos?] each
year and remove [the contents] and give [one third to the]
    priest and
deposit the other two thirds in [the bank so that they may
    be given as a
dedication to the] sanctuary from the offerings, as decided
    by the d[emos].[24]

Again, we find secured sacred storage, whose inventory and proper distribution are overseen by a group of cultic intermediaries, including the priest. This inscription also details human-divine profit sharing and divine-human property distribution mediated both by cultic officials and by the people. Here, though, we also encounter evidence that the god has his own bank on site, which functions, at least in this transaction, to store and funnel divine property for its deployment in the sanctuary. The god is able to control (through those who transact on his behalf) the divine temple business that occurs, without relying on an outside bank. This also means that the *trapezeitai* (bank managers) participate in conducting the god's business in the temple and have equal access to sacred storage.

The third example is a Greek-Latin bilingual inscription from Cyme dating to 27 BCE. It describes the intervention of Augustus and the governor of Asia in a local cult dispute. Following a decree from Augustus and Agrippa that public and sacred places shall be under public or sacred ownership, the inscription details a letter from Vinicius, the governor, demanding action to correct a violation. A citizen named Lysias, citing the temple's outstanding debt, has claimed ownership for the temple, debt, and financial claims of Dionysus in the city. The governor asks city officials to pay off Lysias, writing,

> e(go) v(olo) v(os) c(urare), sei ea ita sunt, utei Lusias quod
> [est] positum pretium fano recipiat et restituat deo fa-
> [num e]t in eo inscreibatur: 'Imp(erator). Caesar deivei f.
>   Augustu[s] re[sti-
> [tuit.]

> I want you to take care that . . . Lysias receives the fixed price for the temple and restores the temple to the god, and that it is recorded on the temple: 'Imperator, Caesar, son of the deified Iulius, Augustus restored it.'[25]

While it is unclear under what circumstances Lysias can claim ownership to the temple, this inscription raises important questions: How much does it cost to bail out a god? How does an individual acquire a god's property, including a temple? How and by whom is the price set to determine how much a god's property is worth? A single inscription cannot answer these questions fully. Yet this text demonstrates that Augustus, a self-described son of a god, intercedes to pay off a religious center's debt holder. In doing so, he "restores" a temple to its god. Gods, a son of god, and humans can participate in financial transactions with one another, and the human can even trade in a god's property; or, we might say, even the god him- or herself can trade or be traded.

God's Funds and Human-Divine Property: Theo-Economics at Jewish Sites

The separation and separate management of divine properties was not limited to Greco-Roman religious persons, and divine involvement in the transactions at sacred sites was not limited to locations with a sacrificial cult. An inscription on a column (225 × 98 cm) comes from a synagogue in Stobi in Macedonia.[26] The column, which was used as spolia for a Christian basilica on the same site, dates from the original synagogue, either to 79 or 163 CE, depending on the reconstruction of a lacuna at the top. This typical dedicatory inscription acknowledges a benefactor, Claudius Tiberius Polycharmus, who has paid for the construction (or perhaps renovation) of his rooms to the "holy place," including the triclinium. It includes several features typical of a dedicatory inscription, including reference to the fulfillment of a vow and the honorific claim that Polycharmus is a father of the synagogue. Polycharmus's gift establishes the synagogue on the ground floor rooms while retaining his ownership and control of the upper floor.[27]

[Κλ(αύδιος)] Τιβέριος Πολύχαρμος, ὁ καὶ Ἀχύριος· ὁ πατὴρ
τῆς ἐν Στόβοις συναγωγῆς ὃς πολειτευσάμενος πᾶσαν
πολειτείαν κατὰ τὸν ἰουδαϊσμὸν εὐχῆς ἕνεκεν τοὺς μὲν οἴκους
τῷ ἁγίῳ τόπῳ καὶ τὸ τρίκλειον σὺν τῷ τετραστόῳ ἐκ τῶν
οἰκείων χρημάτων μηδὲν ὅλως παραψάμενος τῶν ἁγίων, τὴν
δὲ ἐξουσίαν τῶν ὑπερώων πάντων πᾶσαν καὶ τὴν δεσποτείαν
ἔχειν ἐμὲ τὸν Κλ(αύδιον) Τιβέριον Πολύχαρμον καὶ τοὺς {καὶ
τοὺς} κληρονόμους τοὺς ἐμοὺς διὰ παντὸς βίου, ὃς ἂν δὲ
βουληθῇ τι καινοτομῆσαι παρὰ τὰ ὑπ' ἐμοῦ δοχθέντα, δώσει
τῷ πατριάρχῃ δηναρίων μυριάδας εἴκοσι πέντε· οὕτω γάρ
μοι συνέδοξεν, τὴν δὲ ἐπισκευὴν τῆς κεράμου τῶν ὑπερώων
ποιεῖσθαι ἐμὲ καὶ κληρονόμους ἐμούς.[28]

(I) [Claudius] Tiberius Polycharmus, also called Achyrius, the father of the synagogue at Stobi, having lived my whole life according to Judaism, in fulfillment of a vow (have donated) the rooms to the holy place, and the triclinium with the tetrastoa out of my personal accounts without touching the sacred funds at all. All the rights of all the upper (rooms of the building) and the ownership is to be held by me, Claudius Tiberius Polycharmus, and my heirs for all life. If someone wishes to make changes beyond my decisions, he shall give the patriarch 250,000 denarii. For thus I have agreed. As for the upkeep of the roof tiles of the upper (rooms), it will be done by me and my heirs.[29]

This inscription demonstrates that the members of the synagogue, including Polycharmus, understand that the synagogue has its own separate funds, which are designated as sacred. Polycharmus is eager to assert that his funding is from his own property and does not touch those sacred funds. Even though God is not mentioned, it is not difficult to see the similarity between this claim about sacred funds[30] and examples from temple administrations quoted earlier. These funds, while under the control of some synagogue administrative processes, belong to God. Polycharmus also claims that because he has donated his own rooms to the synagogue, he has the right to determine their use in the context of the community and even has the right to demand that a fine be levied if the rooms are used counter to his instructions. This places sacred property under at least partial human control and demonstrates that it is not always the gods who offer divine benefaction to humans.

A second, later, and even more explicit, example comes from a pair of dedicatory mosaic inscriptions found in a synagogue near the ancient harbor in Aegina, which scholars have dated to 300–350 CE.

Θεοδώρου νεω(τέ)ρ(ου) φροντίζοντ(ος) ἐκ [τῆς] προσόδου
τῆς συναγ(ωγῆς) ἐμουσώθη. εὐλογία πᾶσιν ἰσερχ[ο]μένοις.

Θεόδωρος ἀρχισυνά[γωγος φ]ροντίσας ἔτη τέσσερα ἐχ
θεμελίων τὴν συναγ(ωγὴν) οἰκοδόμησα. προσοδεύθ(ησαν)
χρύσινοι π̅ε̅ καὶ ἐκ τῶν τοῦ θ̅ε̅(οῦ) δωρεῶν χρύσινοι ρ̅ο̅.[31]

When Theodorus the younger was phrontistes, the mosaic
was laid down from the revenue of the synagogue. A blessing
on all who enter.

Theodorus, archisynagogos, phrontistes for four years, built
the synagogue from the foundations. 85 gold coins were received, and 105 gold coins from the gifts of God.

The mosaics, set in a tabula ansata, a rectangular frame with han-
dles, on the west end of the floor, with black lettering on a white
background, have no published measurements. The title *phrontistes*,
given to the donor Theodorus (who also serves as the archisynagogos) is attested in Jewish inscriptions from Porto, Rome, Caesarea, and Side; it was broadly used in public administrations in the
late Roman period.[32] Scholars debate what this role specifically did,
whether overseeing communal property, supervising the (re)con-
struction of the building, or serving as the treasurer of the congre-
gation, but the title implies that Theodorus has financial oversight
of the synagogue.[33] Theodorus, who has overseen the building of
the synagogue, dedicates a mosaic paid for from synagogue revenue.
The dedication includes the amounts received from two sources;
the first seems to be some sort of collection from the congregants,
but the second source is from the "gifts of God," which means that
God and the congregants together fund the construction of the
synagogue.

Cultic sites could also serve as places for currency exchange, and
commerce related to cult often occurred within the *temenos* of a sacred site.[34] These transactions meant that money, commodities, and
even persons were bought, sold, and traded. One important example
comes from manumission inscriptions, such as those found at Delphi.[35] The polygonal wall along the sacred way leading to the temple
of Apollo includes some eight hundred manumission inscriptions,
almost all of which date from the second century BCE to the first
century CE.[36] These manumission inscriptions, found on the wall as
well as in the theater, record the process of owners "freeing" their
slaves by selling them to the god Apollo.[37] Manumissions are formulaic and usually include a date of transaction, the price paid, conditions of release (if applicable), witnesses and guarantors for the
transaction, and the agreement between the two parties (the god/

goddess and the slave owner). These sacral manumission inscriptions can also be found in other places in the ancient Mediterranean, including Kalymna, and include a variety of persons participating in a divine-human slave transaction, including persons from a variety of *ethnē*.[38]

One example from Delphi demonstrates the theo-economics at play in divine-human contracts. Inscribed on the polygonal wall of the east terrace of the Treasury of the Athenians in Delphi, it is dated to the late second or early first century BCE. This is a typical *paramonē* (conditional release) inscription, but "this seems to be a rare example of a Jew manumitting a slave in a pagan temple."[39]

ἄρχοντος Ἡρακλείδ[α], μη[ν]ὸς Ποιτροπίου, ἀπέδοτο Ἰο[υδ]-
α[ῖο]ς Πινδάρου, συνευδοκέοντος τοῦ υἱοῦ Πινδάρου, τῶι
[Ἀ]πόλ[λω]νι σῶμα ἀνδρεῖον, ὧι ὄνομα [Ἀμ]ύντας, ἐπ᾽
ἐλευθερίαι, τιμᾶς ἀργυρίου μνᾶν πέντε, καὶ τὰν τιμὰ[ν ἔ]-
χει. βεβαιωτήρ· Κλέων Κευδά[μο]υ. παραμεινά[τω] δὲ
Ἀμύντας παρὰ Ἰουδαῖ[ο]ν, ἕως κα ζῆ Ἰουδαῖος, ποιέων τὸ
ποτιτασσόμενον πᾶν τὸ δυ[να]τόν. εἰ δὲ μή, κύριος ἔστω
Ἰουδαῖ[ο]ς [ἐπι]τιμέων Ἀμύνται ὥς κα φαίνηται αὐτῶι, πλὰμ
μὴ πωλέ[ων]. ἐπ[εὶ δ]ὲ κά τι π[άθ]ῃ Ἰουδαῖος, ἐλεύθερος ἔστω
[Ἀμύν]τας, καθὼς πεπίστευκε τὰν ὠνὰν τῶι θεῶι Ἀμύντας,
ὥσ[τε] ἐλεύθερος εἶμεν καὶ ἀνέφαπτος ἀπὸ πάν[των τ]ὸν
πάντα βίον. εἰ δέ τις ἐφάπτοιτο Ἀμύντα ἐπὶ καταδουλισμῶι,
κύριος ἔστω συλέων ὁ παρατυ[χὼν ὡς] ἐλεύθερον ὄντα,
καὶ ὁ βεβαιωτὴρ βεβαιούτω τὰν ὠνὰν τῶι [θε]ῶι. μάρτυροι·
οἱ ἄρχοντε[ς Νικάτας, Σώ][στρατος, Καλλία]ς, καὶ ἰδιῶται
Τιμοκλῆς, Ξενόκριτος, Σώστρατος, Ταράντινος, Φ[ιλ]-
οκράτης.[40]

In the archonship of Heraclidas, in the month Potropios, Ioudaios (son) of Pindarus has, with the agreement of his son Pindarus, sold to Apollo a male body, Amyntas by name, for five silver minae to set him free and he [Apollo] has the money. Guarantor: Cleon (son) of Cleudamus. Amyntas shall stay with Ioudaios for as long as Ioudaios lives, doing everything he is required to the best of his ability. If, however, Amyntas does not do that, Ioudaios may punish him in whatever way he wishes, but he cannot sell him. If something happens to Ioudaios, Amyntas shall be free, because Amyntas has entrusted the sale to the god he shall be free and immune from any seizure throughout his whole life. If anyone seizes Amyntas to enslave him, let anyone, whoever by chance he is, have the right to rescue him, since he is free, and let the guarantor make the sale to the God secure. Witnesses: the archons Nicatas, Sostratus, Callias, laymen, Timocles, Xenocritus, Sostratus, Tarantinus, Philocrates.

Here Ioudaios and his son Pindarus draw up a contract that sells their slave Amyntas to the god Apollo for the price of five silver minae. The contract has multiple witnesses, some of whom are part of the temple bureaucratic system and others who are *idiōtai* (laypeople). Cleon[41] is named as the *bebaiōtēr* (guarantor) for the transaction, because the contract is not completely fulfilled until Amyntas has continued to serve Ioudaios until the end of his life. Humans serve as participants in this divine-human transaction, and gods and humans are responsible for ensuring its proper enactment and correcting any violations of the contract. In this transaction, while Ioudaios receives the price for his own slave (funded by the slave), Amyntas's ownership is transferred to the god Apollo. While these manumission inscriptions do free (or conditionally free, as is the case here) enslaved persons, the theo-economic rhetoric of manumission contracts suggests that Apollo is a significant slaveholder. He regularly participates in a divine-human slave market with humans acting as witnesses and guarantors to the transactions.

Divine Marketplaces and the Gods of Exchange: Theo-Economics beyond Cultic Sites

Moving beyond cultic sites, the gods can also be found in commercial centers, including in governmental or market *agorai* and *makella*, where fish and sacrificial meat were sold.[42] These spaces were built to maximize proximity and efficiency for intersecting administrative and commercial activity; *makella* in Ostia, Puteoli, Hipponion, and Gigthis were built within a hundred meters of the forum, the *makel-*

lon of Aezani was built near river docks and within a hundred meters
of the agora, and cities such as Perge installed them along the main
road to ease transportation.[43] The architecture or decoration of *makella* often had space dedicated to or reserved for cult, with Mercury
or Hermes as the most frequently honored deity.[44] The genius of
the *makellon* and Fortuna are also often cited, as well as the cult of
the emperor, Neptune, and Liber Pater.[45] The gods also regularly
appear at the point where financial transactions are regulated. A
limestone base from Philippi (65 × 44 × 30 cm), which held a votive
statue, was found to the north of Basilica B, the site of the ancient
makellon. It contains a first-century BCE Latin inscription, which is
also the epigraph to this chapter:

> Mercurio
> Aug(usto). sacr(um).
> Sex(tus). Satrius. C(aii). f(ilius).
> Vol(tinia). Pudens.
> [aed(ilis)][.] Philipp(is).
> [ex mensu]ris. ini-
> [quis aeris p(ondo)] [. . .]

> Consecrated to Mercury Augustus.
> Sextus Satrius Pudens, son of Caius,
> of the tribe Voltinia,
> aedile (?) for the Philippians,
> (erected this altar) out of false measures for the bronze
>   weights.[46]

Here a Roman magistrate, possibly an aedile with oversight of public buildings, consecrates a votive to Mercury Augustus as a site for
the confiscation of false measures. This base likely held a bronze
statue representing Aequitas, which we learn from another similar base from the *makellon* in Philippi.[47] Of this blended imperial-
commercial divinity, Cédric Brélaz writes,

> If these restorations hold, we have here, with inscription
> 117, a second example [in Philippi] of a statue dedication
> to an assimilated divinity of imperial virtues on the part of

an aedile, in addition to the confiscation of false measures. In the present case, the statue was dedicated to Mercury Augustus. The protection of commerce and trade is part of Mercury's attributions. The epithet Augustus which is lent here has the effect of associating the qualities of the divinity with the imperial virtues and suggesting, in return, an assimilation between the emperor and the god. The ordinary values of divinity are thus increased by the imperial aura.[48]

The statue and statue base reveal entanglements of political bureaucracy, imperial cult, and a divine figure associated with commercial activity. This statue might also remind us of the checkbook mentioned in the introduction: the presence of a divine figure is invoked on an object used to complete a financial transaction. By invoking Mercury-Augustus on an object celebrating the confiscation of false measures, this statue reminds persons in the *makellon* that Mercury-Augustus oversees transactions that happen in the space. The presence of Mercury-Augustus, then, also serves as a divine guarantee that the transactions in the space will be measured equitably. This statue literally re-forms any confiscated false measures into the form of a deity, sponsored by an aedile. Human and divine actors intermingle in this center of commercial activity, and persons in the *makellon* might be affected by seeing Aequitas in a variety of ways, including fear, security, or confidence. The gods, including Mercury-Augustus, are actant not only within formal temple spaces but also within the larger economy, even in spaces that we moderns might think of as solely commercial.

The gods were invoked by statues and inscriptions in commercial spaces such as *makella*. Their images were also deployed on coinage, weights, and measurements, the means of and standards for much commerce in antiquity. There is significant evidence of theo-economics on coinage; "coins, which were among the first widely produced publications and reproductions in history, were icons with a value at once spiritual and material, or aesthetic and economic."[49] The issuing authorities themselves, the emperors, frequently represented themselves as gods or sons of gods on their coin issues. These frequent divinization issues cover a wide chronological range, from Tiberius through Constantius II, with relatively standardized imagery and ideology. While the popularity of the imperial cult, with its various temples, priests, and other cultic bureaucracies,[50] varied within the Roman empire, imperial divinization was represented throughout the empire on coins. These coins often include "DIV," "DV," "DIVO," or "CONSECRATIO" in their inscription.[51] A search of the Online Coins of the Roman Empire database run by the American Numismatic Society reveals 288 types with "DIVO," 270 types with "CONSECRATIO," 55 with "DV," and 20 with "DIV."[52] The earliest types are from Tiberius in the early 30s, the latest date to Constantius II, perhaps as late as 361. Most issues are small-denomination bronzes, including *sestercii* during the imperial period, and *nummi* starting with the denominational reforms of Constantine. Divinized imperial figures were nearly ubiquitous on ancient Roman imperial coinage. Imperial divinization coinage represents a particular ideological arc of Roman imperial issues, but gods and goddesses, and other theological imagery, are found on almost all Greek and Roman coin issues. City, provincial, and imperial issuers use divine imagery to invoke local deities in the place of issue, express issuing authorities' virtues such as piety, and intertwine the divinity's authority with that of the issuer.

This is also true in local Philippi issues. One important early example of divinization coinage, an Augustan issue from Philippi, depicts the laureate head of Augustus on the obverse and three bases on the reverse, the middle of which contains a statue of Augustus in military dress.[53] The inscriptions on the obverse and reverse show the entanglements of theological, economic, and imperial ideologies. The obverse includes the legend "*COL AVG IVL PHIL IVSS AVG*," referencing the renaming of the colony at Philippi and Octavian's receipt of Augustus as an honorific; this term identifies him with the role of Pontifex Maximus, mediating between the gods and Roman citizens and colonists.[54] On the reverse, the statue of Augustus labels him as "*DIVI F[ilius]*" next to a statue of the apotheosized Julius, identified by "*DIVO IVL[ius]*." Here, the renaming of the colony is tied to military victory, Octavian's role as divine-human priestly mediator, and his recognition as the son of a god, the apotheosized Julius Caesar. The political message here is powerful. As James R. Harrison notes, "The apotheosized Julius brings victory to his adopted son and vice-regent on earth as the real victor at Philippi."[55]

Because this divine-human interaction occurs on the medium by which financial transactions are conducted, these theological and political claims are suffused through the local economy. This single example of local Philippian issues reveals the complex interplay among humans, gods, divinized emperors, and local history in this colonized city.[56]

With imperial divinization coinage, especially, we see the intertwined theo-economic logics of a ruler who issues coinage to be used for day-to-day economic transactions and who chooses to make theological claims to divinity on that coinage. Thus, the gods not only were participants in economic transactions but also were represented on and understood to authorize the very currency with which much business in the Roman world was conducted. The medium of exchange with which a person might purchase grain or oil was not separate from the watchful eyes of imperial and theological authority.

The weights used to regulate financial transactions also frequently depict both imperial figures and divinities. Weight standards in use from the first century CE well into the Byzantine period take the form of busts of emperors, empresses, or deities such as Hermes/Mercury. These busts hung from steelyards, marked bars along which the weight could slide to help reach the proper measure. Buyers and sellers alike relied on the embodiment of a deity or semidivine imperial figure to set the standard by which accurate and proper measurements occurred. These are precisely the sorts of weights, when counterfeited, which might have been melted down for reshaping into a statue of Aequitas found in the Philippian *makellon*. Imperial figures and divinities occur at many points of transaction, from the currency of the Roman empire to objects like these weight busts, which are used to measure transactions. If you turn to the cover image on this book, you will find one such example: a leaded bronze bust (8 × 6 × 4.7 cm), likely of Nero, which dates from the first century CE.[57]

The theo-economics of coins and weight standards begin to become clearer when we consider a broken limestone table (32 × 196 × 116 cm) that was found in the sanctuary of the Thracian Horseman in Kipia, some fifteen kilometers southwest of Philippi.[58] The table top has two circular cavities, pierced at the bottom and with a molded edge. The table, which was used to regulate measuring standards, would have one or both of the cavities filled with merchandise (such as grain or oil), held in place by a missing mechanism. After the transaction was complete, the merchandise would have dropped to a container below through the hole in the bottom. The table top is inscribed with three brief lines of Latin:

[. . . I]I . uir . s(ua) . p(ecunia) . f(aciendum) c (urauit).
Pro [sa]lute . col(oniae) . Iul(iae) . Aug(ustae) . Philippi-
ens(ium) .
Heroi . A[ulo]nite . sacr(um).

[an unknown] duumvir erected (this table) at his own expense.
For the well-being of the colony Julia Augusta of the Philippiens.
Consecrated to the Thracian Horseman.[59]

This *duumvir*, or joint magistrate who would have been an elite official in the Roman Empire, donates a limestone table for the well-being of the colony at Philippi. This table would have seen regular use in a market setting, measuring merchandise to ensure that transactions were fair and equitable. This *duumvir* consecrates the table to the Thracian Horseman, an important local deity. This measuring table echoes the two statue bases from the *makellon* at Philippi in invoking a deity on objects used for completing transactions. The act of proper measurement served the *salus*, well-being or health, of the colony, and it also was consecrated to a local deity. The commercial transactions that would have occurred on this tabletop were not only commercial transactions. Because of the theological invocations of *salus* and a divinized figure, the transactions were also theo-economic ones.

Imperial and divine eyes watched over transactions that occurred within commercial spaces. The bodies, images, and invocations of gods and imperial god-humans standardized transactions and regulated how much a person could buy, in the medium (currency), measure (weight busts), and process (measuring table) of exchange. The most mundane purchases from oil to grain were also god-purchases.

And human merchants and bureaucrats (including the aedile and *duumvir* from these objects from Philippi and its environs) were expected to regulate their transactions by divinely overseen standards.

Conclusion: Mapping Theo-Economics in Antiquity

Roman economic historians offer helpful analyses to scholars of early Christianity that describe the structure and performance of the ancient Roman economy, offering insights into topics ranging from income distribution to slavery that help situate literature emerging from the earliest Christ followers in the first few centuries CE. Even with the advent of NIE, however, Roman economic historians have not fully been able to integrate religious institutions and practices into their analyses. But scholars of early Christianity have something to offer to Roman economic historians and to the broader field of classics in this regard. With a religious studies framework, and an openness to the ways in which gods are understood as participants in the broader economy, literary and material evidence are able to be analyzed not only as data points for macro-level economics but also as micro-evidence for religious practices that affect the broader economy.

From coins and weights to inscriptions and statues found in commercial spaces to the formal financial bureaucracies of temple banks and storage, the gods pervaded the economic sphere in antiquity. A person participating in any form of financial transaction, from making a purchase in the *makellon* to dedicating an object at a temple to drawing up a lease to participating in a manumission, was likely to encounter the gods, if not as a participant in the transaction itself, then as a figure overseeing that transaction. As we turn to the Letter to the Philippians, we can read the language of gain, loss, abundance, wealth, security, deposit, and prosperity in this context and expect that some of the Philippians would have also had this vibrant range of possibilities of financial interaction with God in mind.

CHAPTER TWO

The Venture of the Gospel

In This Age of Hard Trying, Nonchalance Is Good and
"really, it is not the
        business of the gods to bake clay pots." They did not
          do it in this instance. A few
              revolved upon the axes of their worth
as if excessive popularity might be a pot;

they did not venture the
        profession of humility . . .

—MARIANNE MOORE

"LIVING IS CHRIST AND dying is gain" (Phil 1:21). In this divine accounting, living and dying are given a certain value, set on a spread-
sheet with Christ and gain in the next column. Dying is profitable,
and living is Christ. How much is dying worth? How much is living
worth? And what are the theological and economic consequences—
or, I would say, the theo-economic consequences—of commodify-
ing Christ? Answering these questions requires an analysis of the
Letter to the Philippians for its divine-human financial language.
This language pervades Philippians, including venture, profit, loss,
abundance, need, security, deposits, and partnership. This language
organizes the letter around theo-economic logics.

34

In order to consider the range of this theo-economic language, it is helpful to begin with Phil 1:5–7:

[Εὐχαριστῶ] . . . ἐπὶ τῇ κοινωνίᾳ ὑμῶν εἰς τὸ εὐαγγέλιον ἀπὸ τῆς πρώτης ἡμέρας ἄχρι τοῦ νῦν, πεποιθὼς αὐτὸ τοῦτο, ὅτι ὁ ἐναρξάμενος ἐν ὑμῖν ἔργον ἀγαθὸν ἐπιτελέσει ἄχρι ἡμέρας Χριστοῦ Ἰησοῦ· καθώς ἐστιν δίκαιον ἐμοὶ τοῦτο φρονεῖν ὑπὲρ πάντων ὑμῶν διὰ τὸ ἔχειν με ἐν τῇ καρδίᾳ ὑμᾶς, ἔν τε τοῖς δεσμοῖς μου καὶ ἐν τῇ ἀπολογίᾳ καὶ βεβαιώσει τοῦ εὐαγγελίου συνκοινωνούς μου τῆς χάριτος πάντας ὑμᾶς ὄντας.

[I give thanks] . . . because of your venture in the gospel from the first day until now. I have confidence in this, that the one who began a good work in you will complete it by the day of Jesus Christ. Even as it is right for me to think this way about all of you because I have you in my heart, both in my imprisonment and in my defense and warranty of the gospel, since all of you are my joint-shareholders in grace.

Here, Paul describes himself as being in a *koinōnia* in the gospel with the Philippians (1:5). While this term is often translated as "fellowship," the term has more expansive financial connotations that emerge from a consideration of the epigraphic and papyrological evidence. This evidence, when considered alongside the letter's themes related to finances, opens up a reading of the entire letter within a theo-economic framework. Paul also claims that his imprisonment, particularly his *apologia* and *bebaiōsis*, defense and warranty of the gospel (1:7), is his contribution to the *prokopē*, progress, of that gospel venture. By exploring these terms for their theo-economic valences, the valuation of dying and living that we find in Philippians 1 becomes clearer. A focus on *koinōnia* in Philippians 1 also helps us to consider the use of *koinōnia* in the rest of the letter, particularly in Philippians 4.

At the outset, it is worth noting that some scholars argue that Philippians is a compilation of up to three letters. The compilation position contends that Phil 4:10–20 was at some point a separate letter, perhaps an initial letter of receipt and thanks sent after

Epaphroditus arrived. Phil 1:1–3:1 would then represent a second, more extended letter sent with Epaphroditus upon his return. In this position, the Letter to the Philippians, as we have it, flattens multiple chronological layers in the correspondence between Paul and the Philippian assemblies. Those who argue for the unity of the letter note parallels between various parts of the letter that are identified as belonging to separate fragments. There are, for example, numerous parallels between 1:3–11 and 4:10–20.[1] My focus on theo-economics throughout the letter is not dependent on the letter's unity or composite status. I have chosen to structure my argument here by following the parallels across Philippians 1 and Philippians 4, but the analysis holds whether or not the letter is a unity. In either case, Philippians 1 and 4 are intertwined, whether or not they originally were parts of a singular letter or were sequentially, smaller missives.

Two recent treatments of Philippians reveal the field's continued interest in economic themes within New Testament texts and especially in Pauline materials. In their handling of *koinōnia* language in the letter, both monographs return to regularly asked questions about Paul's compensation and the socioeconomic models of early communities in Christ. They do not address the theological and economic valences of *koinōnia* or the full range of theo-economics in the letter.

David E. Briones takes up the apparent contradictions regarding Paul's financial (in)dependence in 1 Corinthians 9 and Philippians 4.[2] The majority of scholars see Paul's insistence on financial independence and preaching the gospel free of charge in 1 Corinthians 9 as rhetorical overcompensation, given Paul's acknowledgment of receiving financial assistance in Philippians 4. Instead, Briones contends that Paul has a comprehensive financial policy for his communities. Briones argues that Paul receives financial support from the Philippian community because he had a longer, more established arrangement with this group, compared to other *ekklēsiai*, such as that at Corinth.[3] Briones's "socio-theological" approach concludes that Paul, the Philippians, and God are in a complex, three-way relationship based on gift-giving. Yet this "socio-theological" analysis fails to take into account the frequent deployment of *koinōnia* cognates throughout the letter, including in Philippians 1 and 4. The focus on gifts in Briones's book, and its interest in re-creating the social-historical context of the gift language in Philippians 4, results in its glossing over some of the theo-economic complexities of the text, particularly where *koinōnia* cognates are concerned. For all his emphasis on the economic nature of the relationship among Paul, God, and the Philippians, Briones does not address the financial connotations of the term *koinōnia* and its use in Phil 1:5–7.

Briones translates *koinōnia tou euangelion* in Phil 1:5 as Paul's "fellowship in the gospel."[4] According to Briones, *koinōnia* "consists of their [the Philippians'] active participation in contributing to the advance of the gospel, primarily, but not exclusively, through their financial support, which springs from their participation in divine [*charis*]."[5] Although Briones highlights Phil 1:7 as representative of the Paul-God-Philippian gift triangle, by minimizing the financial connotations both here and in 1:5, Briones's analysis cannot account for the pairing in both these verses of *koinōn-* cognates[6] with *euangelion* (gospel). While *charis* is a divine-human resource shared between Paul and the Philippians, in these verses, Paul seems more concerned with describing the gospel by using as an organizing principle the language of *koinōnia*. This minimization of the financial connotations not only of the *koinōn-* cognates but also of the other theo-economic language in Philippians 1 leads to an oversimplified description of the letter's complex articulation of the divine-human relationship as a mere set of gift exchanges. Briones fails to describe the varied ways in which Paul imagines the Philippians as contributing to the gospel venture, and he does not adequately treat the continuation of theo-economic terms into the middle and end of the chapter, where Paul discusses his imprisonment. Briones is instead interested in defending consistency across the Pauline corpus as well as highlighting the importance of gift (*charis*) language in early Christianity.[7]

A second recent work takes up the use of *koinōn-* cognates in Philippians 1 and 4 in order to renew arguments for understanding early Christ communities as similar to Roman *societas*. Julien M. Ogereau's recent philological study of papyrological and epigraphic evidence for the use of *koinōnia*, among other terms, has demonstrated quite convincingly that the cognates of *koinōnia* "essentially expressed the idea of partnership, be it economic, political, marital, or otherwise."[8] This follows in the line of J. P. Sampley's work; Sampley first argued in 1977 that *koinōnia* should be read as equivalent to Roman *societas*. Ogereau argues that these social arrangements, whose primary purpose was to "pool resources, be it human (e.g. slaves, labor), material (e.g. tools, facilities), or financial, towards the fulfilment of a common objective," are helpful *comparanda* for early Christ-following communities.[9] Ogereau's work is also situated in a broader important trend of using evidence from ancient associations as comparanda for the earliest Christ communities.[10] *Koinōn-* cognates are frequently found in business transactions, especially land-lease agreements and other business documents.[11] Ogereau's study helps to demonstrate that "one need not rely on a metaphorical interpretation with which to make sense of the economic discourse [in Philippians]. Rather the evidence suggests that we ought to take it at face value and grapple with the socio-economic dynamics herein implied."[12] Ogereau argues that a number of philological studies were conducted by scholars, especially in the mid-twentieth century, whose ecumenically minded ecclesiological commitments led them away from a financial reading of *koinōnia*. By creating a comprehensive appendix of epigraphic and documentary sources that use *koinōn-* cognates, Ogereau demonstrates that *koinōn-* cognates are used frequently in contractual relationships. Ogereau's study, however, limits its scope to the human-human organization of early Christ communities and thus does not attend to the ways in which his evidence demonstrates that it is hardly unusual for such partnerships, particularly business partnerships, to include a divine-human component in the arrangement.[13]

This contract, from Arsinoite and dating to 52 CE, is drawn from Ogereau's study and demonstrates a typical use of *koinōnia* in business contexts:

καὶ παρέξωμαι ἡμᾶς τόν δαι[14] Κρονι{ων}α καὶ τὸν Παῦσειν ἀπαιρεισπάστους καὶ ἀνεισπράκτους καὶ ἀπαρανοχλήτους κατὰ πάντα τρόπον διὰ τὸ τοὺς τοῦ Τεισένξεως υἱοὺς ἀφανεῖς εἶναι, εἴσους αὐτῶι κο{ι}νωνούς, ὠφειλόντων αὐτῶν πλῖστα δημώσεια

And I shall render you, both Kronion and Pausis, free from hindrance, liability, and impairment, in every way, for the sons of Tisenxsis, who were equal partners in this (property), have disappeared, since they owe much to the public treasury.[15]

This papyrus fragment is a guarantee of immunity offered to Kronion and Pausis in the sale of a property to pay off the long-outstanding debt owed to the public treasury. Two brothers, who had co-owned the property, have left town without settling their public debt. A Ptolemaios offers this document to release Kronion, the notary for the documents of sale, and Pausis, who has purchased the property, from the expense and trouble of future legal liability for the sale. Like many of the examples compiled in Ogereau's appendix, P.Mich. 5.354 describes the participants in the *koinōnia* and lays out the ratio of investment or ownership (here an equal share between the sons). *Koinōnia* arrangements share the potential for both reward and risk. As is clear in this example, the failure of these brothers to pay off their debts has resulted in the forfeiture of their *koinōnia* venture property. Ogereau does well to include epigraphic and documentary evidence, which is frequently overlooked by the majority of scholarship, in his assessment of *koinōnia*. Yet *Paul's Koinōnia with the Philippians* over-corrects against more theologically minded scholarship and thus glosses over evidence that clearly demonstrates that it is hardly unusual for divine beings to be involved alongside humans in *koinōnia* arrangements.

One example, from Ogereau's appendix, reveals the difficulty in trying to disentangle the theo-economics of some *koinōnia* arrangements. At a Nymphaion in Kafizin, in rural Cyprus, numerous pottery fragments and other epigraphic remains dating from approximately 225 BCE provide details of a *koinōnia* that deals in flax and seeds:[16]

χ(άριτ)ι Ἀνδρόκλου κοινονίας τ[ον λ]ίνον καὶ [τοῦ σπέρματος Νὺμφ]ηι τη . . . Ὀνησαγόρας Φιλουνί[υ] δεκατη[φόρος].

By the favor of Androklos's company of flax and seed to the Nymph . . . Onesagoras son of Philounios, the *dekatēphoros*.[17]

The *dekatēphoros* is either the giver or collector of the tithe and thus could refer either to the nymph or to a person who collected and received the tithe on behalf of the nymph, perhaps Onesagoras. Scholars disagree regarding whether Onesagoras is the giver of the tithe from Androklos's business or the go-between who mediates the transaction between the nymph and the *koinōnia*.[18] Whatever the specifics of the arrangement among the *koinōnia*, Onesagoras, and the nymph, it is clear is that a divine being receives the benefits from this business relationship. Whether or not the *koinōnia* sees her as a formal patroness to their flax and seed business, this "family"[19] business considers her worthy of receiving the business's tithe.

From *Paul's Koinōnia with the Philippians*, we have access to an important new data set for considering the ways in which communities in Christ might have heard and understood *koinōnia* and its cognates with contractual valences. Ogereau offers the preceding fragments, and an abundance of other documentary and epigraphic data, as evidence of the dominance of *koinōnia* cognates in describing business and other partnerships in which there is a share in both liability and potential gain. However, he ignores the important, and sometimes explicit, participation of the divine in these partnerships. As with Briones, Ogereau does not account for the theological rhetoric of a *koinōnia* in the gospel. With his project's narrower focus on whether Paul's *ekklēsiai* are equivalent to Roman *societas*, he misses the theo-economic language of the larger letter, in which *koinōnia* discourse dominates.

A Venture in the Gospel

Scholarly questions about Paul's compensation and the poverty of Christ communities have hobbled a comprehensive exploration of the range of theo-economic entanglements throughout the letter. They unnecessarily separate discussions of the implications of Phil 4:15–19, with its clear references to some sort of financial exchange occurring between Paul and the Philippian community, from financial terminology elsewhere in the letter. Instead, all parts of the letter should be subjected to the question: What sorts of human-human and human-divine relationships are described in a partnership between Paul and the Philippians in the gospel?

The very beginning of the letter presents some answers. Paul's stated reason for his traditional thanksgiving is his gratitude "in your *koinōnia* in the gospel from the first day until now."[20] With the term *koinōnia*, Paul describes a business relationship in the gospel, a venture in which both liability and potential reward are shared. The

Philippians have been participants and invested in this joint venture of the gospel from the first day until now.

A comparandum to this sort of *koinōnia* relationship is found in an agreement to a business partnership from Hermopolis, dating to 132 CE, in which Titus Flavius Sarapion agrees to enter a business arrangement with Publius Aelius Apollonius that involves shared land use. After dating the one-year agreement to the seventeenth year of Hadrian, the former writes,

> ἐπὶ τό με τελέσαι τοῦ ἐνελκουμένου σοι φόρου ἢ
> ἐνελκουσθησομένου τὸ ἥμισυ, ἐμοῦ κατ' ἴσον σοι [π]άσας
> τὰς δαπάνας κ(αὶ) σπέρματα κ(αὶ) ἔργα κ(αὶ) {α} τὰ ἄλλα
> πάντα ἀνεμποδίστως ποιησομένου κατὰ τὸ ἥμισυ.
> ἡ κοινωνία κυρία.[21]

> Upon my paying you half of all the tribute that is imposed or shall be imposed, sharing with you equally all the expenditures, seeds, labor, and all other (costs).
> (Let) the partnership (*koinōnia*) be effective.[22]

This typical business agreement details both the shared liability and the object of investment (earlier the inscription mentions Titus's stake in a "half share of the [arable] land")[23] as well as a sense of the timing of the venture. Phil 1:5 does not constitute a written contract or formal written agreement. Yet, as in this papyrus fragment, Paul's pairing of *koinōnia* language with a date ("from the first day") reminds the Philippians of their joint investment in the gospel, and it might have reminded some in the Philippian communities of contract language they would have encountered in other contexts.

Phil 1:6, which also includes a chronological component, both further explains the nature of the *koinōnia* relationship between Paul and the Philippians and complicates that relationship by describing divine involvement. In Phil 1:6, Paul writes

> πεποιθὼς αὐτὸ τοῦτο, ὅτι ὁ ἐναρξάμενος ἐν ὑμῖν ἔργον ἀγαθὸν
> ἐπιτελέσει ἄχρι ἡμέρας Χριστοῦ Ἰησοῦ·

> I have confidence in this, that the one who began a good work in you will complete it by the day of Jesus Christ.

Two other participants in the venture of the gospel are introduced
to the business arrangement: "the one who began a good work," presumably God, and Jesus Christ. The Philippians, then, not only have
a shareholding arrangement with Paul in the gospel but also are, to
some extent, the worksite of that venture. God is described as the
instigator of that work, and Paul, playing the role of absentee site
supervisor, nevertheless expresses his confidence that the work will
be completed on time. The day of Christ is described as the deadline
for completion, without further explanation, but it is clear that the
chronological references bind the two verses together. Paul has had
a *koinōnia* relationship with the Philippians, that relationship is still
active in the present, and this venture is guaranteed continuation
into the future with an agreed-on completion date. The Philippians
themselves are the site of productivity that is expected to bear fruit
for the gospel.

It is difficult to underestimate the importance of Paul's deployment of *koinōnia* language throughout the letter.[24] The term appears
six times in the very brief letter, compared with only two occurrences of *ekklēsia*. In Philippians, Paul uses *koinōnia* discourse instead of *ekklēsia* discourse, which is more prevalent in other letters,
including 1 Corinthians. The three-to-one *koinōnia*-to-*ekklēsia* ratio found in Philippians might not seem significantly imbalanced at
first. However, the context of the two appearances of *ekklēsia* help
to demonstrate that the term is supplanted by Paul's deployment of
koinōnia cognates.

Ekklēsia occurs at Phil 3:6 and Phil 4:15. In Phil 3:6, in the midst
of an autobiographical section in which Paul talks about his reasons
for "confidence in the flesh" (Phil 3:4), he adds, "according to zeal,
a persecutor of the *ekklēsia*." Here, Paul's pursuit of the assembly is
buried in a long list that includes Paul's circumcision on the eighth
day as well his affiliation with the *genos* of Israel and the tribe of
Benjamin. This first deployment, then, is a reference to Paul's past
and has no immediate connection to the Philippian community, its
context, or the larger rhetorical framework of the letter. The second
appearance, in Phil 4:15, occurs in the passage that has vexed scholars with concerns about Pauline compensation. There he writes,

οὐδεμία μοι ἐκκλησία ἐκοινώνησεν εἰς λόγον δόσεως καὶ
λήμψεως ἐι μὴ ὑμεῖς μόνοι.

No assembly invested with me in the matter of giving and receiving except you.

Here, while Paul acknowledges that the assemblies with which he corresponds commonly call themselves *ekklēsia*, he only refers to the Philippian *ekklēsia* in order to compare it with other assemblies with which he had contact when he came out of Macedonia. The central term in this clause for understanding Paul's relationship with the Philippian community is *ekoinōnēsen*, another *koinōnia* cognate. The dominant image of this phrasing is a business partnership for which Paul has kept proper track of "receipts and expenditures,"[25] not a democratic civic assembly.[26]

Anna Miller's recent book *Corinthian Democracy: Democratic Discourse in 1 Corinthians* helps set out the potential differences between what she terms *ekklēsia* discourse of 1 Corinthians and what I mean by theo-economic *koinōnia* discourse of Philippians. Regarding 1 Corinthians, Miller writes,

> Paul's rhetorical aim . . . is marked by rhetorical tactics drawn from a robust discourse of democracy—what I term "*ekklēsia* discourse"—a discourse pervasive in the eastern Roman Empire and within the Corinthian community. . . . Paul's rhetoric is inscribed with this *ekklēsia* discourse in order to make his own leadership legitimate in a context where the same discourse was being mobilized to construct a community around the actions of empowered, free citizens. . . . [I] trace a persuasive ancient discourse of democracy that emerged out of the Greek civic institution composed of the body of free citizens, the *ekklēsia*. . . . This ancient Christian community was constructed, at least rhetorically, as a civic and political body. . . . Disparate community members at Corinth took a vocal role in deliberative decision making within this Christian community.[27]

Ekklēsia discourse, when deployed by Christ followers in Corinth, marks a community as a civic and political body. The rhetoric of *koinōnia* in Philippians instead imagines a financially bound body. These ties extend beyond the long-term human-human partnership in giving and receiving that we find in Philippians 4, as well as the financial and labor support that the Philippians seem to offer to Paul in prison, to imagine a divine-human financial and theological entanglement that includes the Philippians; Paul; his cowriter Timothy; Epaphroditus, whom the Philippians sent to aid Paul; Christ; and God. There is a venture in the gospel, overseen by God and due by the day of Christ, to which all must contribute.

Ogereau has helpfully demonstrated that *koinōnia* discourse is pervasive in the Greco-Roman world as terminology deployed in business contracts, legal documents, and other agreements that involve shared risk and reward. Therefore, Paul's rhetoric inscribed within this *koinōnia* discourse should be examined for the ways in which he legitimates his own contributions to a gospel venture in a context in which, because of his imprisonment and his continued receipt of financial support, he could be seen as not contributing to, or perhaps even causing loss to, the gospel venture. And when Paul constructs this ancient Christ-following community as a theoeconomic body, he not only asserts himself as the ultimate broker between the Philippians and God in the gospel venture but also leaves open the possibility for this community to understand itself as having a share in contributing to the gospel venture.

Paul's Deposit and the Progress of the Gospel Venture

At the end of Philippians 1, Paul discusses his chains. Scholars have long wondered about the location and nature of Paul's imprisonment. Phil 1:12–18 contains important evidence for identifying the location of the composition of the letter, mapping out Paul's travels, and assessing the fit between Paul's letters and the narrative presented in Acts. Key to these arguments about location are an interest in Paul's statement in 1:13 that his "imprisonment in Christ has become known to the whole praetorion," because Paul's use of the word *praitōrion* might help decode the location of the letter's composition.[28] Scholars have argued that Philippians was composed in a Roman prison,[29] in Ephesus,[30] or in Caesarea.[31] Although Craig S. Wansink has concluded that "speculating about where Paul may have been imprisoned when he wrote Philippians and Philemon, although enjoyable and intriguing, leaves us with little more than

enjoyable and intriguing speculation,"[32] scholars nevertheless continue to focus on these verses as a way to get at questions of Pauline
biography and timeline. Acts does not seem to provide an answer;
Angela Standhartinger has recently noted that "the image [of Paul's
imprisonment] drawn in Acts is historically implausible."[33]

Wansink's monograph on the subject of Paul's imprisonments
reveals the difficulty in reconstructing ancient prison experiences.
Wansink advocates for an examination of Paul's rhetoric about his
imprisonments instead of attempting to reconstruct the historical
situation of his imprisonment. Literary and documentary sources
about ancient prisons are chronologically scattered and fragmentary, and many sources on prisons (e.g., early Christian martyrdom
texts) postdate Paul. Archaeological evidence of prisons is scarce and
often disputed.[34] What is clear, however, is that Paul does not reference several common literary tropes about prison that are found in
other ancient sources,[35] including references to darkness,[36] smell,[37]
and overall poor living conditions.[38] Instead, Wansink compares
the rhetoric in Philippians with other epistolary evidence, focusing
on Cicero's *Ad Quintem Fratrem* 1.3.[39] While his summary of the
evidence and rhetoric about ancient prisons is helpful, Wansink's
conclusions are mostly limited to an exploration of the connection
between the gift in Philippians 4 and the imprisonment rhetoric in
Philippians 1. The specter of concern for Paul's receipt of financial
support from the Philippians continues to loom, limiting the set of
questions that have been brought to this passage in particular and
the framing texts of the letter as a whole.

I submit that we can read Paul's discussion of his imprisonment
in Philippians 1 instead as a continuation of the theo-economics of
a *koinōnia* in the gospel. Paul has just finished describing his relationship as a *koinōnia* in the gospel under the supervision of God,
a venture in which both Paul and the Philippians share the potential for both reward and risk. Ogereau's work has demonstrated that
this language is economic, and my own analysis earlier has shown
that this is also, at the same time, theological. We find divine beings
participating in precisely these types of contractual relationships.
A *koinōnia* in the gospel would have been legible because here, as
elsewhere, theology and economics are inseparable. Paul writes in
Phil 1:12,

Γινώσκειν δὲ ὑμᾶς βούλομαι, ἀδελφοί, ὅτι τὰ κατ' ἐμὲ μᾶλλον
εἰς προκοπὴν τοῦ εὐαγγελίου ἐλήλυθεν

I want you to know, brothers and sisters, that the things that
have happened to me have happened for the success of the
gospel.

Recall that Paul and the Philippians participate together in the
theo-economic context of the gospel venture in which risk and reward are shared. If the Philippians' contribution to the gospel venture is as a worksite of God (1:6), a contribution that will be completed by the day of Christ, Paul, as the worksite supervisor, the one
who makes supplication to God on their behalf, is ensuring that they
will yield a fruitful harvest of righteousness (1:11) and contribute an
abundance of love in knowledge and discernment (1:9). Paul's discussion of his own imprisonment, then, is his proffered contribution
to the success of the gospel venture in which he is partnering with
the Philippians.[40]

The use of *prokopē*, or progress, here, is a clue to the continuation of the contractual language that comes before. *Prokopē*, regularly translated as "advancement" or "progress," also has connotations of success and prosperity. It also regularly occurs in contracts
and letters related to business. One example is a letter from the early
second century CE written from a Dionysius to Theon with instructions about their farming:

Διον[ύσιο]ς Θέωνι τῶι {τῶι} τιμιωτάτ(ῳ) χαίρειν.
εὖ ποιήσεις ἐπάν σοι δόξῃ ἵνα τὰ κτήνη τοῦ Φαβίου
παραμείνῃ εἰς τὴν ιβ ὅπως ἄρξωσι τῆς χλοροφαγίας τῇ ιγ.
τοῦτο γὰρ ἔδοξέ σοι [ἵ]να καὶ τὸ κατατιθέμενον
    λαχανόσπερμον
προκοπη[ν] σχῇ τῶν ποτισμῶν πρὸ χλοροφαγία[ς].
Κόμισαι λαμψάνας δέσμας ἕξ [. . .] ἐπὰν οὖν παραγένῃ δύνῃ
    ἐφειδῖν αὐτούς.
δὸς τὴν πισσα Καρφιλᾷ καὶ τὸ ἀγγῖον τῶ(ν) περιστερεώνων
    καὶ τὸ λεπτίον.
κέλευσον δοθῆναί μοι χάρτην. ἐρρῶσθαί <σε> εὔχο(μαι)
    τιμιώτατατ(ε) . . .

Dionysios to his esteemed Theon, greetings.

See to it, if you think best, that the cattle of Fabius remain with you until the 12th in order that they may begin their pasture-feeding on the 13th.

For this was your idea, that the vegetable seed that has been sown may have advantage of the progress of the irrigation, before the grazing.

Bring six bundles of charlock [. . .] Accordingly, when you come you can examine them.

Give the saddle-pack to Philas, and the crock of the dovecotes, and also the cloth. Order papyrus to be given to me. I pray for your health, most esteemed . . .[41]

Dionysus writes this brief letter to Theon asking him to keep the cattle of a third party, Fabius, until a certain date in order that they then begin cattle grazing. Dionysus reminds Theon that this would help them follow his initial idea to leave the seed extra growth time in irrigation before grazing the cattle. After a few more instructions to bring some items, give some others to Philas, and order papyrus, the letter closes. Here we see that part of the business of both farming and cattle rearing is a complex process that requires careful timing and juggling multiple responsibilities. Dionysus pens a brief letter to address the minutiae of planning, crossing the physical distance that lies between the two and making sure the cattle are raised, the seeds are given time for irrigation, and papyrus is ordered.

Paul, too, is crossing the distance from prison with a reminder of the *koinōnia* in the gospel that he and the Philippians share. Given the agricultural imagery of the Philippians providing a harvest as God's worksite, Paul is making the claim that the things that have happened to him, namely, his imprisonment, are actually a contribution to that shared responsibility for the gospel. Paul reminds the Philippians to grow so that they might yield a full harvest, and he also assures them that his imprisonment, too, is part of the shared project in the gospel venture. The Philippians might have been concerned that the gospel venture, in which they had invested financially and spiritually, was delayed, or even at risk, from Paul's imprisonment. Paul assures them that his imprisonment actually upholds his part of the partnership because it brings progress (*prokopē*) to the gospel.

If we take seriously the papyrus land lease of Sarapion or the inscribed Nymphaion votive at Kafizin quoted earlier, in which *koinōnia* is deployed to talk about co-ownership, we see that Paul and the Philippians share in a particular business of the gospel. Paul's imprisonment, so he asserts, contributes to the success of that venture. Such an interpretation is further bolstered by a scattering of legal and financial connotations: Paul's first mention of his imprisonment in Phil 1:7 as in the defense (*apologia*) and security (*bebaiōsis*) of the gospel. This is certainly legal rhetoric, as many scholars have noted. Most scholars, influenced by Adolf Deissmann, read both terms in a legal context without financial overtones; *apologia* is read as the defense speech, while *bebaiōsis* is also read legally as positive proof claims.[42] *Bebaiōsis*, however, is also an important theo-economic term; its context is not formal legal terminology but business and contract language. As Angela Standhartinger has noted, the term belongs to the "contexts of philosophy, oaths, and the language of business, [and] means the solidifying or confirmation of promises, statements, or knowledge previously uttered. . . . There is no forensic usage of the word apart from Phil 1:7."[43] Given the theo-economic context of the gospel venture, it makes sense to take *bebaiōsis* in the context of its nearly ubiquitous use in contracts to suggest warranties or securities in business transactions. A typical example from 144 CE details an extract from the contract for a sale of a camel:

(hand 3) Ταουῆτις Ἁρπαγάθου μετ[ὰ κ]υ[ρ]ί[ο]υ
τοῦ συγγενοῦς Στοτοήτεως τοῦ
Στοτοήτεως ὁμολογῶ πεπρα[κέ]ναι
τῷ Σαταβοῦτι τοὺς ὑπάρχοντ[άς] μοι
[καμή]λους δύο θηλίας ἐσφραγισ-
μένας κατὰ τοῦ δεξιοῦ μηροῦ νῦ [. . .]
καὶ ἦτα ταύτας τοιαύτας καὶ ἀπέχω
τὴν τιμὴν ἀργυρίου δραχμὰς
πεντακοσίας καὶ βεβαιώσω πά-
[σῃ βε]βαιώσι καθὼς πρόκιτ[αι]
[. . .] ἔγραψα ὑπὲρ αὐτῆς
(hand 4) ἐντέτακ(ται) διὰ γρ(αφείου) Σοκνοπ(αίου) Νήσου).

I, Taouetis, daughter of Harpagathes, with her guardian, her kinsman, Stotoetis, son of Stotoetis, acknowledge that I have sold to Satabous two female camels belonging to me, marked on their right thigh with Ny and Eta, on the spot, just as they are, and that I have received the price of five hundred drachmas and I shall guarantee with every guarantee, as aforesaid.
I, [Sykos, son of Neilos], wrote on her behalf.
[break] (m. 4) (The contract) was registered through the grapheion of Soknopaiou Nesos.[44]

Taouetis guarantees not only that the transaction has occurred but that she has received the proper price and provided the camels that have been described. Taouetis, as the seller of the camels, is the one offering the guarantee that the terms of the transaction have been met and both the type and quality of the camels and acknowledging receipt of payment. The larger contract includes a date of transaction, marking time by imperial year. Satabous, the buyer, is named elsewhere in the contract as responsible for registering the camels and paying any taxes that might be owed, and the contract is written down for Taouetis by a scribe, who also witnesses the contract. If the Philippians understand the gospel as a *koinōnia*, Paul's invocation of a *bebaiōsis* might have reminded them of this ubiquitous language found in contracts across the ancient world.[45]

Guarantees were offered for a variety of transactions, from camel sales to land leases, and they also were sometimes offered when the contract involved the sale of human beings. One example from 140 CE in Alexandria is a bill for final payment on the purchase of a young girl named Sarapias:

[. . .] [μετὰ κυρίου τοῦ]
δεδομένου μοι κ[ατὰ τὰ Ῥωμαίων ἔθη]
Σέξστου Πομπη[είου] [. . .]
Πτολεμαίου [τραπεζίτῃ χαίρειν· χρη-]
μάτισον Κασ [. . .] τοῦ Κεφάλωνος
Σωσικοσμείῳ τῷ καὶ Ἀλθαιεῖ τειμὴν δούλης
Σαραπιάδος ἐνγενοῦς Ἀλεξανδρείᾳ τῆς

καταγεγραμμένης μοι ὑπὸ αὐτοῦ κατὰ δί-
πλωμα Ἑλληνικὸν ἁπλῷ χρήματι καὶ οὔσης ἐκτὸς ἱερᾶς νόσου καὶ ἐπαφῆς ὥστε
ἀπέχειν αὐτὸν τὰς ὅλας τῆς τειμῆς ἀργυρίου
δραχμὰς χειλίας, σὺν αἷς ἔχει διὰ χειρὸς
ἀργυρίου δραχμαῖς ὀκτακοσίαις τὰς λοιπὰς
ἀργυρίου δραχμ(ὰς) διακοσίας, βεβαιοῦντος
τοῦ ἀδελφοῦ αὐτοῦ Ἰσιδώρου Σωσικοσ-
μείου τοῦ καὶ Ἀλθαιέως, (γίνονται) (δραχμαὶ) σ. (ἔτους) γ
Αὐτοκράτορος Καίσαρος Τίτου Αἰλίου Ἀδριανοῦ
Ἀντωνείνου Σεβαστοῦ Εὐσεβοῦς Ἐπεὶφ ιθ.
(hand 2) Κας [. . .]

[So-and-so, with the kyrios] granted me [in accordance with Roman usage], Sextus Pompeius [. . . , to so-and-so] son of Ptolemaios, [banker, greeting.] Pay to Kas[sianos . . . son of so-and-so, grandson] of Kephalon of the Sosikosmeian tribe and the Althaian deme, as the price of a slave, Sarapias, born in Alexandria, who has been conveyed to me by him in accordance with a Greek double document, simpla pecunia and as being free from the sacred disease and epaphe, so that he may have the complete thousand silver drachmas of the price, when added to the eight hundred silver drachmas which he has through hand, the remaining two hundred silver drachmas (= 200 drachmas), his brother Isidoros of the Sosikosmeian tribe and the Althaian deme acting as guarantor. Year 3 of Imperator Caesar Titus Aelius Hadrianus Antoninus Augustus Pius, Epeiph 19. (2nd hand) I, Kas[sianos . . .][46]

A woman has sent to a banker named Sextus Pompeias an enslaved person named Sarapias, with an agreed-on total sale price of one thousand drachmas. The woman has eight hundred drachmas from Sextus Pompeias but is still owed two hundred, so she sends out a bill requesting the outstanding balance, invoking not only the buyer but the guarantee (*bebaiōsis*) over the sale offered by the buyer's brother Isidoros. The bearer of the bill, Kassianos, is tasked with obtaining payment from Sextus and, if necessary, the other individual who can be held liable for payment: the guarantor, Isidoros. The text is crossed out in two strokes, so the order seems to have been canceled (or perhaps completed). Here papers, people, and payment traveled back and forth, and a person served as the guarantor of the proper completion of a still outstanding contract. In the case of the *koinōnia* at Philippi, news of Paul's guarantee to the Philippians may have come via the labor of Epaphroditus, with perhaps instructions to continue to solicit the financial support that might represent their "fruit" and contribution to the gospel venture. The Letter to the Philippians, like this incomplete sale, represents an ongoing relationship with outstanding obligations.

When Paul claims that his imprisonment offers a *bebaiōsis*, a guarantee, of the success of the gospel venture, he reminds the Philippians that he is the one who brought the *koinōnia* in the gospel to them. In the contract language between Paul and the Philippians (overseen by God), Paul is the seller who is able to instigate its guarantee. Paul is responsible for assuring the Philippians of the terms of that gospel venture, and he includes his own imprisoned body as the guarantee of that contract. The Philippians, who have previously partnered with Paul in giving and receiving and who have probably given him support while in prison, still owe the yield of the fruit of righteousness by the day of Christ Jesus. Paul's contribution comes through his imprisoned body (Phil 1:20). Paul, as the instigator of the contract, also offers his own guarantee that through his imprisonment (rather than in spite of it), the gospel venture will continue to succeed.

To take one last, late example, we find a contract for the lease of irrigation equipment on a papyrus fragment dated to August 311 CE. Three women who own a vineyard lease out the maintenance of the irrigation systems on a third of the land to Pereitis, who agrees to maintain the vineyard and its irrigation in exchange for a share of the wine and of the proceeds from the dates and fruits grown on the property. In the contract, Pereitis seeks to reassure the vineyard owners that he will complete any necessary maintenance on time:

[. . . καὶ ἐπιδέχομαι] μισθώσασθαι ἐπὶ ταῦτα ἔτη δύο ἀπὸ τοῦ
αὐ[τοῦ] ἰσειόντος

[κ (ἔτους) καὶ η (ἔτους) . . .] γεωργουμένων τω χωριω καὶ τῶν
    ἐνόντων φοινίκων [. . .]
[. . . ὁ] λόκληρον παρὰ τῷ προκειμένῳ Ἀπφοῦτ[ι] ὃς γεωργήσει
[ἀκίνδυνα πάντα παντὸς κινδύνου. β]αιβαιωμένης δέ μοι τῆς
    ἐπιδοχῆς ἐπάναγκες ἐπιτελέσω
[τὰ ἔργα πάντα τῷ δέοντι καιρῷ] καὶ τ[ὸ]ν πο[τισ]μὸν καὶ τὰ
    ἄλλα εὐκαίρως καὶ ἐπὶ τέλει τοῦ [χρ]όν[ο]υ [πα]ραδ[ώσω]
[τὴν ἄμπελον ἐπι]μεμελημένην τοῖς ποτισμοῖς καὶ τὰ φυτὰ
    ζωγονοῦντα [καὶ] εὐθαλο[ῦντα]
[διὰ παντός, γεινομέν]ης ὑμῖν τῆ[ς] πράξεως παρά τε ἡμων
    καὶ ἐκ τῶν ὑπαρχόντων μοι πάντων
[κυρία ἡ ἐπιδοχὴ καὶ ἐπ]ε[ρ]ω[τη]θεὶς ὡμολόγησα. ὑπατε[ί]ας
    τῆς προκιμένης μη(νὸς) Μεσορὴ ἐπαγ(ομένων).
[Αὐρ(ηλία) . . . ἔσχον τούτ]ου τὸ ἴσον. (hand 2) Αὐρή(λιος)
    Σερῆνος καὶ ὡς χρ(ματίζω) ἔγραψα ὑπὲρ αὐτῆ[ς
    γρ(άμματα) μ]ὴ εἰ[δυίας].

[. . .] and I undertake to lease for these two years from the
incoming 20th and 8th year . . . cultivating the lots and the
. . . in the presence of the aforesaid Apphous which he shall
cultivate, everything guaranteed against any risk. When this
undertaking is secured to me I will of necessity accomplish
all the operations at their proper time, without delay and
everything done at the proper time, and at the end of the period I shall return the vineyard cared for with the irrigations
and the plants living and flourishing always, and you have
the right of execution against me and against all my property. The undertaking is normative and after having been
formally questioned I have agreed.[47]

Guarantees are also a way of offering assurance in an ongoing financial relationship in which the risk might be lopsided. Here, Pereitis
is in a financially more unstable position; he needs to lease the land
(and the oxen to help work the land) and manage a complex irrigation system in exchange for a portion of the wine and produce the
land yields. The owners have the power in this relationship, and
the task of maintaining the vineyard incurs some risk for them if
Pereitis's end of the contract is not withheld. Without proper maintenance, for example, the land might not yield a full harvest, or the

vines and trees could be harmed. The owners might have a better yield if they lease the land to another worker. These uneven power dynamics help explain why Pereitis offers a triple assurance that all necessary work will be done at the proper time, without delay and, just to make sure the point is clear, at the right time. These assurances reflect an anxiety that comes from Pereitis's position as the person with less negotiating power in the contract.

Paul, too, offers extra assurances. He reminds the Philippians that, despite his unstable position, he is offering a full guarantee for the gospel. The Philippians, too, will yield a full harvest of righteousness at the proper time, and Paul's contribution through his own imprisonment guarantees the overall prosperity of the gospel venture and therefore also the Philippians' proper yield. Paul, like Pereitis, is in a position of seemingly less power; he is and has been receiving support from the Philippians, and he is imprisoned. But by shifting the focus to the Philippians as God's vineyard, Paul attempts to return himself to the position of power vis-à-vis the Philippians; they are the agricultural worksite that needs to yield a harvest as their contribution to the gospel.

As Paul describes his imprisonment as a secure deposit left for the prosperity of the gospel venture, he leaves open the question, How, exactly, does imprisonment contribute a guarantee to that venture? The phrasing suggests the possibility that Paul understands his own imprisoned body to be object of security or deposit. This becomes even clearer later in Phil 1:16:

οἱ μὲν ἐξ ἀγάπης, εἰδότες ὅτι εἰς ἀπολογίαν τοῦ εὐαγγελίου κεῖμαι.

Some [proclaim Christ] out of love, knowing that I am deposited for the defense of the gospel.

Here, Paul is laid up or "deposited" (*keimai*) in prison for the defense of the gospel. He is rendered passive in his situation. This idea continues in Phil 1:20, where Paul claims,

ἐν οὐδενὶ αἰσχυνθήσομαι, ἀλλ᾽ ἐν πάσῃ παρρησίᾳ ὡς πάντοτε καὶ νῦν μεγαλυνθήσεται Χριστὸς ἐν τῷ σώματί μου, εἴτε διὰ ζωῆς εἴτε διὰ θανάτου.

In no way will I be tarnished/shamed, but in all boldness
of speech as always and even now Christ will be magnified (*megalunthēsetai*) in my body, whether through life or
through death.

Paul "objectifies" himself as an object deposited in prison, and he
argues that this deposit is his contribution to the gospel venture
and that, despite opposition, his imprisonment will bring about the
success of that venture. *Keimai* is a flexible term, used for both people and objects, and often includes financial valences when referring
to objects.[48] Paul has already rhetorically blurred the human-object
line at the outset of the letter; he and his cowriter Timothy call
themselves "slaves of Christ" (Phil 1:1).[49] Given Paul's claim to be
a slave of Christ, the reference to magnifying Christ in his body
(*megalunthēsetai*), and the theo-economic language that pervades the
rest of Philippians 1, it makes sense to read Paul's use of *keimai* along
a human-object spectrum. Paul's imprisoned body magnifies Christ
and profits the gospel venture. The Philippians' continued support
of Paul in prison (through sending Epaphroditus and other financial support) is a contribution to a warrantied object that is placed
exactly where it needs to be to for the success of the gospel venture.

But in antiquity, did people deposit things and expect a profit
out of the transaction? And were the gods involved in the business of
object storage and secured transactions? Beate Dignas writes about
items deposited for storage in temples and sacred places, explaining,
"There is no doubt that depositing an object in a temple or sacred
place transformed it into the god's property. Even when votive offerings of silver and gold were damaged and melted down, the new
objects or even ingots were kept in the temple and continued to be
recorded as such. What had once been dedicated was to remain in
the sanctuary."[50]

Evidence from Greek and Roman banking systems indicates that
the line between deposits and loans is deeply blurred and that temples and divine beings are involved in the business of profit-turning
storage. Two legal concepts, the Greek *parakatathēkē*[51] and the Roman *depositum irregulare*, indicate the long-term deposit of goods
that included the expectation of a return on investment. The Greek
parakatathēkē is a deposit agreement in which the person receiving

the deposit is able to return the deposit in similar species, or even sometimes in items of comparable value, rather than the actual goods deposited. This allows the institution or individual receiving the deposit to reinvest those items through loans on interest, trade, or other business transactions. For example, if an individual deposited a certain amount of coinage or a certain weight of grain, the person who holds the storage could trade or loan those specific items out to others and return to the depositor equal base value of other items without obligation to return the specific items.[52] The Roman *depositum irregulare*, attested in Justinian's *Digest*, continues this legal concept, although some legal scholars question whether the two are exact parallels. Both types of transactions are widespread in antiquity.[53] The arrangement is supposed to be a benefit to the depositor, because she or he is providing goods to the depositee that can be reinvested elsewhere, so a profit is expected; and the differences, if any, with other loans in antiquity, seem to lie in which parties retain or release ownership of the goods being deposited.

In the Artemis temple at Sardis, an inscription details the content of a *parakatathēkē* agreement between a wealthy individual and Artemis. Found in two columns on the walls of a room identified for temple storage, it dates to approximately 200 BCE. The inscription is engraved on a white marble block (0.88 × 2.745 × 0.82 m) on the face of the north wall.[54] It is a detailed deposit-loan arrangement, explicitly using the term *parakatathēkē* to describe the contract. Also, while the temple wardens are responsible for the administration of the transactions, the agreement has been made between Mnesimachus and the goddess Artemis herself. Mnesimachus had received a deposit on loan of some of Artemis's property, and when the temple wardens approach to recoup the deposit, Mnesimachus is unable to supply the full amount. He offers his properties, including land, buildings, and slaves, as *bebaiōsis* (security) until he pays back the amount owed from the deposit. The second column of the inscription offers these details:

[. . .] μηθ]ὲ[ν ἐξέστω μή]τε ἐμοὶ μήτε [τοῖς ἐμοῖς ἐκγόνοις
    μήτ]ε [. . .]
μήτε ἄλ(λ)ωι μηθενὶ μηκέτι ἀπολύσασθαι· καὶ ἐάν τις
    ἐμποιῆται ὑπέρ τινος τῶν κωμῶν ἢ τῶν κλήρων
ἢ ὑπὲρ τῶν ἄλλων τῶν ὧδε γεγραμμένων ἐγὼ καὶ οἱ ἐμοὶ
    ἔκγονοι βεβαιώσομεν καὶ τὸν ἀντιποιούμενον
ἐξαλλάξ(ο)μεν, ἐὰν δὲ μὴ βεβαιώσωμεν ἢ παρὰ τὴν
    συγγραφὴν παραβαίνωμεν τήνδε γεγραμμένην
ἐπ[ὶ] τὰς κώμας καὶ τοὺς κλήρους καὶ τὰ χωρία καὶ τοὺς
    οἰκέτας ἅπαντας εἰς τὰ Ἀρτέμιδος ἐχέτωσαν,
καὶ οἱ νεωποιοὶ ὑπὲρ τούτων ἐκδικαιούσθωσαν καὶ
    κρινέσθωσαν πρὸς τοὺς ἀντιποιουμένους
ὡς ἂν βούλωνται, καὶ ἐγὼ Μνησίμαχος καὶ οἱ ἐμοὶ ἔκγονοι
    ἀποτείσομεν εἰς τ(ὰ) Ἀρτέμιδος
χρυσοῦς δισχιλίους ἑξακοσίους πεντήκοντα, καὶ ὑπὲρ τῶν
    γενημάτων καὶ τῶν καρπῶν
ἐὰν μὴ καρπεύσωνται ἐν ἐκείνωι τῶι ἔτει εἰς τὰ Ἀρτέμιδος
    ὁπόσου οὖν χρυσίου ἄξια ἦι καὶ ταῦτα
ἀποδώσομεν, καὶ τῶν οἰκοδομη(μά)των καὶ φυτευμάτων τῶν
    τῆς Ἀρτέμιδος ἢ ἄλλο τι ὅ τι ἂν ποιήσωσιν
ὅσου χρυσίου ἄξια ἦι τὴν ἀξίαν ἀποδώσομεν, μέχρι δὲ ὅσου
    μὴ ἀποδῶμεν ἔστω ἡμῖν ἐν παρακαταθήκηι
τέως ἂν ἅπαν ἀποδῶμεν. . .

Neither to me [nor to my heirs, nor . . .] . . .
nor to anyone else any longer the right of redemption.
    Should any person lay claim to any of the villages or of
    the allotments
or to the other things here specified in writing, I and my
    heirs will act as warrantors and will oust the claimant.
If, however, we shall fail so to act, or if we shall commit any
    breach of the contract hereby drawn up
in respect to the villages and the allotments and the lands and
    all the slaves, these shall remain the property of Artemis,
and the temple-wardens shall on account of the same con-
    duct legal proceedings and obtain judgment against the
    claimants
in any way that they may see fit; and I Mnesimnachus and
    my heirs will pay to the treasury of Artemis

2650 gold staters; and on account of the produce and of the
    fruits,
should the temple-wardens receive no fruits in that year, we
    will further pay to the treasury of Artemis such sum in
    gold as the same may be worth;
and the value of the buildings erected and of the lands
    brought under cultivation by Artemis, or of such other
    things as the temple-wardens may do,
whatever the same may be worth in gold, we will pay; and so
    long as we shall not have paid, the debt shall constitute a
    deposit-loan owing by us
till we shall have paid the whole amount . . .[55]

This example demonstrates that the lines between deposits and loans
in antiquity are blurry and that divine beings involve themselves in
the business of contracts involving guarantees. This inscription also
demonstrates that providing someone with a commodity that they
can dispose of, redistribute, or otherwise use as they will is a normal
transaction but is one in which a profit is expected. The gods are often involved in these transactions, and the goods exchanged are not
limited to currency but also include property, future crops, and even
enslaved persons. Artemis is heavily involved in this contract; her
treasury is the repository for the funds owed by Mnesimachus, land
properties under temple control are described as being cultivated by
Artemis, and the temple wardens serve as her broker in enforcing
Mnesmimachus's payoff of the owed amount.

     While I am not trying to argue that Paul presents his impris-
onment as a formal *parakatathēkē* agreement, the *koinōnia* in the
gospel in which Paul and the Philippians are invested belongs to
God's property. Paul has just described the Philippians as the land
property of God (Phil 1:6), a property that bears fruit (1:11) for
the gospel venture and on behalf of which Paul is the one to make
supplication to God. Paul, as the slave of Christ (1:1), is deposited
in prison for the profit of the gospel venture in which he and the
Philippians are involved, and therefore he argues that he contributes
to the venture despite his situation of imprisonment and his receipt
of financial support from them—a situation because of which one
could reasonably argue that he is not contributing.

A reading of the theo-economic language of this passage also helps to explain some of the phrasing in Phil 1:21–24 that has puzzled commentators who focus exclusively on Paul's *apologia* of the gospel, overlooking the theo-economics in the text. In Phil 1:21 and the beginning of 1:22, Paul writes,

Ἐμοὶ γὰρ τὸ ζῆν Χριστὸς καὶ τὸ ἀποθανεῖν κέρδος. εἰ δὲ τὸ ζῆν ἐν σαρκί, τοῦτό μοι καρπὸς ἔργου, καὶ τί αἱρήσομαι οὐ γνωρίζω.

For me, living is Christ and dying is gain. For if I am living in the flesh, this is a fruitful work for me, and I do not know what I prefer.

If Paul understands his imprisoned body as a physical contribution to the gospel venture, with this language and the verses preceding it, he indicates a willingness to be disposed of or redistributed for the success of that venture. This is why, for Paul, whether living or dying, Christ is magnified or exponentially grows (*megalunthēsetai*) in his body (1:20).

Even in the midst of this passive, self-objectifying language, Paul adds that although he desires to depart and be with Christ, "to remain in the flesh is more necessary for you [the Philippians]" (1:24). While Paul blurs the line between person and object, as an imprisoned and invested body, he continues to assert that he is making contributions to the gospel venture and that the Philippian *koinōnia* requires his contribution to succeed. In this way, Paul continues to assert his authority over the Philippians in the gospel venture as the ultimate broker with God, the key to the gospel's success.

How does Paul's seeming indifference to living and dying match with his confidence that the situation will work out for his *sōtēria*? In Phil 1:19, Paul writes,

οἶδα γὰρ ὅτι τοῦτό μοι ἀποβήσεται εἰς σωτηρίαν διὰ τῆς ὑμῶν δεήσεως καὶ ἐπιχορηγίας τοῦ Πνεύματος Ἰησοῦ Χριστοῦ

For I know that this will turn out for my security through your supplications and through the supply of the spirit of Jesus Christ.

In Phil 1:19, the word *epichorēgia* (supply) cues us to recognize the theo-economic logics at play. The spirit of Jesus Christ is a provision that, combined with the supplications of the Philippians' support, will help Paul's imprisonment turn out for his *sōtēria*. Given that Paul immediately transitions to claiming that *sōtēria* will occur whether or not he lives or dies, we should not read *sōtēria* as indicating some personal confidence in Paul's deliverance from prison. Instead, *sōtēria* seems to have physical, theological, and economic components. Paul is the object deposited in prison; his placement there supports the gospel venture in life or in death. If this is the case, then his *sōtēria* seems to be about the physical security of the value of the deposit and not about the physical well-being of Paul's body. Living magnifies Christ, and dying would also prove profitable. Thus, *sōtēria* also seems to be about Paul's value to the gospel, which is provided for by the Philippians' support and the provisions of the spirit. This commodifies Paul's suffering and potential death as a contribution to the venture of the gospel, and *sōtēria* is worthy of further support and investment, whether from the Philippians or through the spirit of Jesus Christ.

A Divine Promissory Note in Philippians 4

A consideration of the theo-economic valences of a *koinōnia* in the gospel in Philippians 1 also opens up a way of reading Philippians 4 that considers not only the human-human financial relationship between Paul and the Philippians but also the human-divine financial relationships that are frequently overlooked in scholarly analysis of the passage. I end with this chapter because Philippians 4 has drawn significant attention from scholarship interested in Paul and his relationship with the *koinōnia* at Philippi. It gives clues to the situation(s) behind the letter(s) sent back and forth between Paul and the Philippian communities. Philippians 4 also offers evidence for the financial relationship between Paul and the Philippians, but scholars have not sufficiently read it in light of Philippians 1's theo-economic language and thus have missed some of the human-divine financial dynamics at work.

Three topics have been especially popular. First, Paul's mention of having received a gift (*to doma*) has received significant attention, in the context of a growing interest in conventions of gift exchange in antiquity.[56] Gifts in antiquity imply unequal power relations, and patronal gifts to clients allow patrons to assert power over their clients. Even within associations pooling resources, some members often exert power over others through patronage as part of a broader social system of reciprocity.[57] Some scholars, such as Gerald W. Peterman, have argued that Philippians 4 represents Paul's attempt to counteract these dynamics. Despite having received gifts from the Philippians—a situation that might put him in the client position—Paul reminds the Philippians that their gifts have been to God, not him.[58] Second, scholars have considered this thank-you letter as a resource for mapping the social status of the persons mentioned: Euodia, Syntyche, Clement, and Epaphroditus. Scholars such as Joseph Marchal have been interested in situating "Euodia, Syntyche, and Epaphroditus in the social conditions of Philippi and, in doing so, [discerning] the forms of social stratification in the developing assembly community."[59] These women and men, some of whom may have been enslaved or freedpersons, help scholars to understand the networks of early Christ followers in Philippi.[60] Third, Philippians 4 speaks openly of hunger, lack, and need, and scholars have used it to think about the ways in which the members of the Philippian communities, despite their poverty, participated in generosity and abundance.[61] These scholarly foci on human-human interactions have raised important observations. But my interest in Philippians 4 lies elsewhere, in the ways in which theo-economic rhetoric has been deployed to marshal authority in those human-human financial transactions through a divine-human economy, brokered by Paul.

In Phil 4:15, Paul acknowledges that when he set out from Macedonia,

οὐδεμία μοι ἐκκλησία ἐκοινώνησεν εἰς λόγον δόσεως καὶ λήμψεως εἰ μὴ ὑμεῖς μόνοι

no assembly ventured with me in the matter of giving and receiving except you alone.

Here, again, we find a cognate of *koinōnia*—this passage offers the best evidence for what Julien Ogereau argues is the formal financial relationship between the Philippians and Paul.[62] Ogereau argues that the phrase "in the matter of giving and receiving" is Paul's attempt to translate the Latin *ratio dati et accepti*, a ledger of monies or goods given or received.[63] The Philippians seem to have gone all-in investing early in the gospel with Paul by partnering in giving and receiving. Here Paul acknowledges this support, using the language of a formal receipt. Since the beginning, the Philippians have invested in the financial networks among Christ-following communities that were under Paul's management.

This giving seems to have been above and beyond what Paul might have expected; the Philippians were angel investors.[64] The Philippians have also provided additional support more recently, by sending Epaphroditus to Paul during his imprisonment and by sending items along with him. Paul, in his imprisonment, somewhat reluctantly acknowledges both Epaphroditus's labor and the additional things that he has received from Epaphroditus, and Paul classifies these using the language of sacrifice. As Laura Nasrallah has recently noted,

> The Philippians are rendered grammatically passive in their role of contributing to Paul by means of Epaphroditus. Yet Epaphroditus can be considered an active part of the financial aid package actively offered by the Philippians, not merely the bearer of that aid. Elsewhere in the letter, Paul makes Epaphroditus's life and labor part of the accounting relations between himself, the Philippians, and God. We read in Phil 2:30 that Epaphroditus "nearly died for the work of Christ (τὸ ἔργον Χριστοῦ), venturing (his) soul in order that he might pay your deficiency toward me (ἀναπληρώσῃ τὸ ὑμῶν ὑστέρημα τῆς πρός με λειτουργίας)" (2:30; see vv. 25–30).[65]

Instead, Paul focuses on what he has received from the Philippians. Paul calls these gifts in Phil 4:18 "a fragrant offering, an acceptable sacrifice, pleasing to God."

Scholars have largely considered whether these two instances of giving—Epaphroditus's recent support and the earlier partnership between the Philippians and Paul in giving and receiving—indicate long-term programs of financial support between the Philippians and Paul. These instances are perhaps in contradiction to 1 Corinthians 9, where Paul claims that he does not accept financial support and preaches the gospel free of charge.[66] Yet few scholars have noticed the way in which Paul reorients this human-human financial interaction into the broader theo-economy mapped out both in Philippians 4 and throughout the letter.

As Paul reorients the Philippians' giving as directed not toward him but toward God and as he frames that support within the language of sacrifice, he redirects benefit of the gifts received away from himself and toward God. As Thomas R. Blanton, IV, notes, "Paul presents himself as a proxy or broker between the Philippians and Israel's god. . . . By portraying gifts to himself as gifts to God, Paul evades any implication that donations made to him should reduce him to the level of a client or dependent."[67] What began as help to Paul, probably within a frame of patron-client relations, is reframed under a broader theo-economy in which giving to God, like sacrifice, is an act of pious obligation. Giving in return is a necessary response to divine beneficence.

Even though Paul is the one who is fulfilled by Epaphroditus and the gifts he brings in Phil 4:18, Paul continues to style himself as a vessel for the divine gospel venture who does not need the support he has received because he has learned the secret of both plenty and lack (Phil 4:12). Paul uses sacrificial language to describe what Epaphroditus brings on behalf of the Philippians. This sacrificial language is tied to the ways in which Epaphroditus's labor is a part of the sacrificial process. After all, Epaphroditus is named as a *leitourgos*, a term usually used for someone serving within the context of a cult. "This turn of phrase sacralizes whatever the 'need' is that Paul has. Likely a slave or freedperson, Epaphroditus's labor was useful to Paul, as was the slave Onesimus's."[68] On the one hand, Paul's acknowledgment of Epaphroditus's role in bringing the sacrifice recognizes his importance within the Christ-following community; his leadership is essential to the sacrificial giving that Paul acknowledges here. However, the broader divine economy that Paul maps out still places the giving of the Philippians within a network of human obligation to the divine. Giving (including giving to Paul) is generous but also necessary; it is a part of the sacrificial system.

The Philippians' giving, even if it is carried by the labor of Epaphroditus, is channeled through Paul, God's ultimate broker to the Philippians.

Bringing a theo-economic framework to the chapter also draws our attention to two other phrases that are commonly overlooked. First, in describing the ways in which the Philippians sent support to Paul when he was in Thessalonica, Paul reassures them:

> οὐχ ὅτι ἐπιζητῶ τὸ δόμα, ἀλλ᾽ ἐπιζητῶ τὸν καρπὸν τὸν πλεονάζοντα εἰς λόγον ὑμῶν

> Not that I sought the gift, but I sought the fruit that accumulated to your account. (Phil 4:17)

Paul describes a divine-human economy in which all transactions are tallied up. The Philippians have an open account with God, and their giving, mediated through Paul, is recorded in the divine register. This fruit (*karpon*) in 4:17 also echoes the harvest language of Philippians 1, in which Paul promises the Philippians that they will yield the harvest (*karpon*) of righteousness that is through Jesus Christ for the glory and approval of God (Phil 1:11). The way that the Philippians add to their divine account, the way in which they demonstrate the fruit of their righteousness, comes through their giving. Instead of marking the benefits Paul has received from the Philippians, he focuses instead on the benefits accrued to the Philippians. The Philippians' generosity is profitable giving, because it is all tabulated within their divine account.

How do we know that Paul has in mind a divine account and is not simply working within the formal human-human financial arrangement of a patron-client relationship? In Phil 4:19, right after using sacrificial language (itself a human-divine transaction) to acknowledge the Philippians' most recent support, Paul claims,

> ὁ δὲ Θεός μου πληρώσει πᾶσαν χρείαν ὑμῶν κατὰ τὸ πλοῦτος αὐτοῦ ἐν δόξῃ ἐν Χριστῷ Ἰησοῦ.

> My God will fill all your lack according to his riches in glory in Christ Jesus.

Paul acknowledges that the Philippians' giving is not a light sacrifice but is also a real hardship: "this giving hurt."[69] If the sacrificial giving that the Philippians have sent to Paul has incurred too much loss, Paul stakes the claim that God will fill up their lack with divine wealth. God is wealthy enough to provide for any lack the Philippians may have, no matter how much they have given. Paul uses the singular possessive here; this is Paul's God. This is a divine promissory note, which Paul is able to call in as God's broker. Paul may be the recipient of financial benefit from the Philippians, but the Philippians will be the recipients of theological benefits that will be supplied by God in glory in Jesus Christ. Wealth is not only counted in terms of financial support or human labor but in terms of divine wealth, glory, righteousness, and Christ Jesus. Paul understands all of the Philippians' support—from their earliest investment to the labor of Epaphroditus to their support during his imprisonment—not only in terms of his financial arrangement with them but also in terms of God's role in that relationship.

We find language of abundance and lack regularly invoked to discuss divine-human relationships. Sometimes, the divine is understood to have a role both in providing for successful harvest and also in balancing the financial loss or windfalls that can arise in agricultural ventures. A proclamation of Hadrian, dated sometime after May 31, 136 CE, offers a tax abatement following a year of poor Nile flooding:

Αὐτοκράτωρ Καῖσ[αρ, θεοῦ Τραϊανοῦ Παρθικοῦ υἱός, θεοῦ
    Νέρουα]
υἱω[ν]ός, Τραιανὸς [Ἀδριανὸς Σεβαστός, ἀρχιερεὺς μέγιστος,]
δημ[αρ]χικῆς ἐξουσ[ίας τὸ κ, αὐτοκράτωρ τὸ β, ὕπατος]
τὸ γ, πατ[ὴρ πατρίδος λέγει·]
καὶ νῦν ἐνδεέστ[ερον ἀναβῆναι τὸν Νεῖλον, ὡς καὶ πέρυσι,]
πυθόμενος οὐδὲ τ [. . . εἰ καὶ τοῖς προτέροις ἔτεσι ἑξῆς οὐ
    τελείαν μόνον,]
ἀλλὰ κ[αὶ] μείζω [σχεδὸν ὅσην οὔπω πρότερον ἐποίησα-]
το τὴν ἀνάβασιν [καὶ πᾶσαν τὴν χώραν ἐπελθὼν]
αἴτιος [ὑπ]ῆ[ρ]ξεν αὐ[τὸς τοῦ πλείστους καὶ καλλίστους
    καρποὺς]

ἐξενεγ[κεῖν], ὅμω[ς ᾠήθην ἀνάγκην εἶναι ποιήσασ-]
θ[α]ί τινα [πρὸς] τοὺς [γεωργοὺς φιλανθρωπίαν, καίτοι]
προσδοκῶν--σὺν θ[εῷ δὲ εἰρήσθω--τῶν ἐπιόντων]
ἐτῶν, καὶ εἴ τ[ι] νῦν ἐ[νεδέησεν, ἀναπληρώσειν καὶ αὐτὸν]
[τὸν Ν]εῖλον καὶ τὴν γῆ[ν...τη...εξοτερων τὴν φύσιν τῶν
    πραγ-]
μάτων, ὡς ἐγ μὲ[ν εὐροίας καὶ πολυκαρπίας εἰς ἔνδειαν]
[μ]εταβαλεῖν, ἐγ δὲ τῆς [ἐνδείας εἰς ἀφθονίαν. τύχῃ δὲ τῇ
    ἀγα-]
[θ]ῇ·

Proclamation of the Emperor Caesar, son of the deified
Traianus Parthicus, grandson of the deified Nerva, Traianus
Hadrianus Augustus pontifex maximus, holder of the Tri-
bunician Power for the 20th time, imperator for the second
time, consul thrice, father of his country; Having been informed that even now, just as last year, the Nile has risen
rather deficiently . . . , even considering the fact that during
the preceding years successively its rise was not only plenti-
ful, but rather almost higher than any time before, and that,
flooding all over the country, it caused the produce of abundant and beautiful crops, still I have deemed it necessary to
bestow a favour on the cultivators, although I hope—this
be said with God!—that in years to come any possible deficiencies will be supplied by the Nile itself and the earth,
according to the revolving (?) nature of things, changing
from prosperous flow and abundancy to scarcity, and from
scarcity to plenty. For good luck![70]

The rest of the proclamation details the specifics of the tax abatement. Residents from different areas are offered three- to five-year
delays in tax payments to find time and income to make up for lost
yields.

In this proclamation, divine presence suffuses the political and
agricultural system. Hadrian describes himself as a son and grandson of gods, as father of the country, and as *pontifex maximus*. A son
of a god controls the divine-human tax system in which humans are
obligated to pay regularly from the yield of their harvest. Moreover,

this son of a god invokes God to ask for the Nile and the earth to supply any deficiencies in the harvest yield. Hadrian partners with God in offering favors to those who are responsible for producing a harvest (*karpon*). Hadrian can provide short-term relief, but he calls on God to ultimately fulfill the harvest that allows the broader divine-human theo-economic tax system to return to its regular cycle, supported by the Nile. As with the Letter to the Philippians, we find language of fulfillment (with cognates of *plēroō*) paired with agricultural language to describe a system that on the surface may look like a simple human-human financial relationship: taxes. This tax relief reflects a much broader theo-economic system in which humans have theo-economic obligations and are also dependent on divine favor to provide for the harvests to meet those obligations.

Paul is no emperor. Yet this comparandum allows us to see more clearly that Paul is encouraging the Philippians to understand their giving as part of a larger theo-economic system in which they have both divine obligation and the promise of divine reward. Paul presents himself as keeping the divine accounts for the Philippians, and he receives their gifts so that he can tally up their harvest yield for God. He reminds them that their sacrificial giving, even if it has led to their lack, will be paid off by the wealth of God, who always settles on outstanding accounts. The payment they can expect to receive might not come in the form of a better Nile flood season, as with the Hadrian proclamation. Paul is not offering a form of the prosperity gospel, in which financial giving leads to financial prosperity. Rather, Paul describes divine wealth in terms of glory and Christ Jesus. This alternative theo-economy will somehow still fulfill the Philippians' need. Paul offers a divine guarantee because, despite his protestations to the contrary in Phil 1:7, he cannot offer any human guarantee in his imprisonment that he will be able to pay them back directly for the financial support he has received.

Intersecting with this divine accounting and divine promissory note, we see that Paul commodifies suffering in Philippians 4. So too, in Phil 1:12, Paul offers his own suffering as his contribution to the gospel; in Phil 2:30, Epaphroditus's illness while laboring for Paul has put his own life at risk to make up for the Philippians' deficiency; and in Phil 3:10–11, Paul understands himself in a profitable partnership in suffering with Christ in order to achieve righteousness and resurrection from the dead.[71] In Phil 4:14, Paul offers the Philippians a partnership (*sunkoinōnia*) in affliction (*thlipsis*). Paul allows the Philippians a share in the venture of affliction, and their contribution comes through their giving. In fact, the difficulty of their giving is precisely what gives them a share in the larger venture of affliction. For Paul, of course, it cannot compare to his own larger contribution that comes from his hard giving—after all, this is not a venture in equal shares but is Paul's *thlipsis*. Thus, we should read Paul's purported obsequiousness and reluctance over receiving financial support alongside his insistence that the Philippians' abundant generosity, even to the point of painful giving, is only a share in Paul's own affliction. Even in a letter of thanks, Paul continues to try to broker God.

Conclusion: The Value of Living, Dying, and Giving

By considering the ubiquity of *koinōnia* in contractual language, we see that we should read a *koinōnia* in the gospel as a venture in which the Philippians and Paul share in risk and reward. Reading Philippians 1 with a focus on *koinōnia* helps us explain language found throughout Philippians 1, including the claim that "living is Christ and dying is gain" (Phil 1:21). Paul's description of his imprisonment as happening for the *prokopē*, or progress, of the gospel (Phil 1:12) should then be read within the theo-economic context of the gospel venture in which Paul and the Philippians participate. Paul first mentions his imprisonment at Phil 1:7 by claiming that it is in the defense (*apologia*) and security (*bebaiōsis*) of the gospel. Unlike commentators who, following Adolf Deissmann, have tried to pair *bebaiōsis* with *apologia* as a formal legal term, I have argued that it makes the most sense to take *bebaiōsis* in the context of its use in contracts to suggest warranties or securities in business transactions. Securities can be both physical property and persons (often slaves are lumped together with other properties in securing loans). Read in this light, Paul's claim that his imprisoned body is his contribution to the success of the gospel venture is legible. In circumstances in which the Philippians are providing support, including probably financial support, for Paul during his imprisonment, Paul could have been perceived as causing loss to the gospel venture. To offset that perception, Paul, who identifies with Timothy as a slave of Christ at the letter's opening, claims to be the security for the success of the gospel venture. In doing so, Paul continues to assert himself as a mediator between God and the Philippians in the gospel venture, because only he can guarantee the gospel's success through his imprisonment. Thus, the confidence that Paul's situation will turn out for *sōtēria* means that *sōtēria* has physical, theological, and economic components. A focus on *koinōnia* in Philippians 1 also helps add an additional layer of analysis to recent scholarship on Philippians 4. In Philippians 4, we find that Paul's acknowledgment of financial support from the Philippians is couched within a broader divine-human economic system in which Paul and the Philippians both have divine obligation and the promise of divine reward.

CHAPTER THREE

The Christ Commodity

Father, part of his double interest
Unto thy kingdom, thy Son gives to me,
His jointure in the knotty Trinity
He keeps, and gives to me his death's conquest.

—JOHN DONNE, "THE HOLY SONNETS"

A *Koinōnia* in Suffering

IN CHAPTER 2, WE saw the ways in which theo-economic language pervades the Letter to the Philippians, especially Philippians 1. Understanding the financial valences of *koinōnia* allows us to see that Paul understands himself in a contractual relationship with the Philippians under divine supervision. If we consider the theological and financial implications of a *koinōnia* in the gospel, the reasons for Paul's use of theo-economic language to describe his imprisonment become clearer. Paul claims his imprisoned body is his contribution to the gospel venture in circumstances that might be seen as causing loss to the gospel.

We also find a *koinōnia* cognate in Philippians 3. In this chapter, Paul is the partner in a venture of suffering with Christ. What are the implications of using a theo-economic term to describe suffering (*pathēmata*)? To answer this question, I map out the theo-economic implications of a venture in suffering in Philippians 2–3 by focusing in particular on a cluster of financial terms in Phil 3:7–11. In these verses, not only is suffering valued using contractual language, but Christ too is commodified.[1] In Phil 3:8, in the midst of a passage rich in theo-economic language, Paul describes a divine tally sheet in which he counts all of his gains as loss "so that he might gain the profit Christ." The divine becomes imbued with financial valuation that can be measured in accounting terms as well as bought, sold, and traded. This phrasing also raises questions about divine-human resources and who controls access to them. Is the divine or access to it a resource that can be tallied? What resources do the gods, as economic actors, control? Do some control more than others? Are humans, whether through sacrifice or other forms of piety, the ones who control the gods' access to resources? We find theo-economic language not only in the way that Paul describes the Christ followers of Philippi and their joint investment in the gospel but also in reflections on theological resources that may at first seem surprising: righteousness, resurrection, and the meaning of suffering.

By considering divine-human resources, this chapter maps out the complex system of divine accounting in antiquity in which humans, the gods, and even economic systems themselves are viewed as actants. The gods, on the one hand, control both earthly and heavenly resources, from land and money to health and salvation.[2] On the other hand, humans control the physical and theological resources on which the gods depend, from piety to the food and drink of sacrifice. And, as we find in a passage such as Phil 3:7–11, sometimes divine figures are themselves the resources. I compare the accounting language of Phil 3:7–11, in which Paul describes a theological accounting system in which Christ is a profitable resource, to a variety of literary and epigraphic comparanda, including Lucian's *Lives for Sale*,[3] a text in which humans and gods participate in the purchase of human/divine figures. A theo-economic system exists in which access to the gods and the gods themselves become understood as commodities that can be bought, sold, and traded.[4] Our analyses of economics in antiquity should not only consider typical questions of access to and control of resources such as land, food, water, and money but should also begin to address questions about access to and control of theological resources such as salvation and resurrection from the dead.

The Christ Commodity: Theo-Economic Language in Philippians 3:7–11

The financial language that we encounter in Phil 3:7–11 can help us begin to be more attentive to divine participation in these theological and economic entanglements.

[Ἀλλ᾽] ἅτινα ἦν μοι κέρδη, ταῦτα ἥγημαι διὰ τὸν Χριστὸν ζημίαν. ἀλλὰ μενοῦνγε καὶ ἡγοῦμαι πάντα ζημίαν εἶναι διὰ τὸ ὑπερέχον τῆς γνώσεως Χριστοῦ Ἰησοῦ τοῦ Κυρίου μου, δι᾽ ὃν τὰ πάντα ἐζημιώθην, καὶ ἡγοῦμαι σκύβαλα ἵνα Χριστὸν κερδήσω καὶ εὑρεθῶ ἐν αὐτῷ, μὴ ἔχων ἐμὴν δικαιοσύνην τὴν ἐκ νόμου, ἀλλὰ τὴν διὰ πίστεως Χριστοῦ, τὴν ἐκ Θεοῦ δικαιοσύνην ἐπὶ τῇ πίστει, τοῦ γνῶναι αὐτὸν καὶ τὴν δύναμιν τῆς ἀναστάσεως αὐτοῦ καὶ [τὴν] κοινωνίαν [τῶν] παθημάτων αὐτοῦ, συμμορφιζόμενος τῷ θανάτῳ αὐτοῦ, εἴ πως καταντήσω εἰς τὴν ἐξανάστασιν τὴν ἐκ νεκρῶν.

But whatever was for me a gain, these things I calculated as a loss on account of Christ. But even more I calculate that all things are a loss on account of the better value of the knowledge of Christ Jesus my Lord, on whose account I counted all things as a loss, and I considered them dung, so that I might gain the profit Christ and be wealthy in him, not having my righteousness that is from the law but that is through faith in/of Christ, which is a righteousness from God in faith, in order to know him and the power of his resurrection and a venture in his sufferings, being conformed to his death, if somehow I might attain resurrection from the dead.

In this brief passage, cognates of five different accounting terms appear, some of them more than once: *kerdos* (gain), *zēmia* (loss), *huperexō* (to exceed), *heuriskō* (to acquire wealth, to fetch or earn money),[5] and *koinōnia*. While a few of these terms have a range of meanings, *kerdos* and *zēmia*, the core terminology of the logic in these verses, have no meaning apart from the financial. It is therefore unnecessary to turn to documentary and epigraphic evidence of *kerdos* and *zēmia* to explore their financial connotations, as I did in chapter 2. Instead, considering the use of such overtly financial terms in Philippians 3 alongside other literary texts that use similar language of gains and losses to think about divine-human relationships deepens our contextual understanding of an ancient world in which gods were actant in the ancient economy and financial language was useful to the ancient theological imaginary.[6] This cluster of up to eight financial terms within a brief four verses describes a theological exchange. Paul highlights two resources that he possesses in abundance: markers of Jewish status and knowledge of Christ. Phil 3:7–11 tally these resources on a sheet of divine accounting, in which Paul sets the exchange rate for the knowledge of Christ; at the high rate he sets, only he seems to have enough on hand to make that exchange.

How is this theological exchange calculated? Paul tallies all of his reasons for confidence in the flesh into a single gains column. In Phil 3:7, he moves these gains to a loss column; Paul reckons all assets as losses because of the surpassing value of the knowledge of Christ Jesus. Paul says he counts these former gains as worthless excrement (*skubala*) so that he might gain the profit Christ (*Christon kerdēsō*). *Kerdēsō* implies turning a profit, and Christ as the object of the verb is the profit that Paul acquires. For Paul, acquiring Christ is profitable, even if the assets that must be exchanged amount to everything that might be considered valuable. Christ is figured as an object of investment for whom Paul will exchange everything. The Christ commodity allows Paul to participate in a *koinōnia* with Christ in suffering and to attain resurrection from the dead.

The exchange that Paul describes is a theo-economic accounting system in which you only have or gain what you are willing to lose or devalue. This upends several expectations of good commercial practices. First, in this theo-economic accounting system, profits are really losses, and losses are profitable. While accounting language is used, this accounting system is topsy-turvy. Second, in this system, the radical exchange that counts all things as a loss inflates the value of Christ. The exchange pushes the value of knowledge of Christ, and Christ himself, higher. Because Paul begins this accounting with his own reasons for confidence and because the accounting rules set forth only allow you to gain what you devalue, only Paul has the right kinds of statuses on hand to devalue. Philippians 3, which contains polemical language at its outset, combined with Paul's list of reasons for confidence that he is willing to set aside, creates a theo-economic exchange in which Paul has the most status currency to hand over for Christ. Knowledge of Christ requires so much devaluation that only Paul seems to have enough on hand to complete the transaction. Third, the use of *skubala* indicates how much Paul devalues all of his reasons for confidence. This extreme self-devaluation makes possible his acquisition of Christ as the ultimate profit.

The use of financial terminology clustered in Phil 3:7–11 has not drawn scholarly attention, and analyses have often focused on tying these verses to the broader project of filling in details of Paul's biography and connecting the passage to the conversion story of Acts 9. The use of *termini technici* from the commercial world is often passed over as vaguely metaphorical, and the complex logics and implications of the proposed exchange have not been fully disentangled. F. F. Bruce serves as an example: "To know Christ and to gain Christ are two ways of expressing the same ambition. If Christ is the one 'in whom are hidden all the treasures of wisdom and knowledge (Col 2:3)' to know him means to have access to those treasures, but to know him for his own sake is what matters to Paul most of all. . . . To gain Christ means to be found in him, to enjoy faith-union with him."[7] Bruce, mixing metaphors, turns to theo-economic language elsewhere in the Pauline tradition in his own description of these verses but chooses a comparandum that does not quite match up. As a result, he ignores the commodification of Christ found in Philippians 3 and spiritualizes the exchange described here in a way that focuses on knowledge of Christ (Phil 3:8) and faith in Christ (Phil 3:9) without full treatment of what it means to gain Christ as a profit.[8]

To take another example, L. Gregory Bloomquist highlights the inclusio bound by *kerdos* and *kerdēsō*, as well as the parallel phrasing using *zēmia*. Rather than explore the financial valences of these terms, he describes "Paul's purpose [as] highlighting the term [*skubala*] . . . by leaving that term uncomfortably isolated and stark: any allegiance to [*sarx*], as opposed to *Christos*, is simply useless garbage.

Thus Phil 3:7–8 brings Paul to the conclusion of his argument in-
augurated in 3:3, namely, to the [*en Christōi*] pole of the contrast."[9]
Bloomquist highlights the contrast inherent in these verses without
exploring the fact that the primary rhetorical vehicle for discuss-
ing in Christ identity in these verses is through financial language.
Bloomquist is hardly alone in emphasizing anything but these terms
in the passage. While some scholars such as Bloomquist and Bruce
see these verses as a straightforward description of Paul's "spiritual"
conversion and Christology, the Christology implied by describing
becoming a Christ follower using the language of a financial exchange is hardly straightforward.

Even scholars interested in economic themes in Philippians have
not fully explored the cluster of financial terminology in Phil 3:7–11.
Julien Ogereau's recent book nowhere directly addresses Phil 3:7–
11, because of the book's focus on "investigating one of Paul's strategies to finance his missionary activities" through an examination
of the socioeconomic dimensions of Paul's *koinōnia* with the Philippians.[10] Ogereau is interested in the ways in which the financial valences of *koinōnia* provide evidence for the financial relationship between Paul and the Philippians. Since Phil 3:7–11 does not directly
relate to disputes over the exact nature of that human-human financial relationship, Ogereau leaves it aside. However, one of the six
occurrences of *koinōnia* in the letter is, as we have seen, in Phil 3:10,
when Paul writes that he is in a partnership in Christ's sufferings
(*koinōnian pathēmatōn autou*). But what are the theo-economic dimensions of Paul's *koinōnia* of suffering with Christ?

David Briones's recent project focuses on Paul's financial policy
with his communities, trying to solve apparent inconsistencies between 1 Corinthians 9 and Philippians 4 about questions of Pauline
compensation.[11] Briones argues that there is a three-way gift-giving
relationship among Paul, the Philippians, and God and that divine
charis (grace/gift) is the primary gift that affects the relationship between Paul and the Philippians. So even though Briones does address intersections of theology with finance in the letter, he largely
overlooks Phil 3:7–11 and the commodification of Christ.[12] It is difficult to map out the theo-economic logics of Phil 3:7–11 without
an acknowledgment that the control and distribution of resources
does not simply include human-human financial interactions but

also theological resources. These theological resources are not limited to *charis* (grace/gift)[13] but include suffering, resurrection from the dead, and even Christ. Phil 3:7–11 does not neatly fit into Briones's three-way gift-giving model.

Exploring other philological comparanda helps to describe the ways Phil 3:7–11 both plays with and upends the expectations of commercial transactions, accounting practices, and price setting. Governmental authorities, from local governing bodies to the emperor, frequently intervened in the minutiae of markets, and these interventions are memorialized not only in the bureaucratic paperwork often preserved on papyrus but also in public inscriptions. *Zēmia* and *kerdos* are frequently found in these types of documents to mark standards and boundaries for appropriate business interactions. One such intervention comes from the emperor Hadrian, preserved in an inscription found on two white marble fragments. Fragment A was found at the eastern end of the north portico in the lower market of Pergamon, a commercial center for the city, while Fragment B was reused as spolia in a Byzantine church.[14] The inscription, dated to 130 CE, preserves an imperial letter that sets regulations for currency exchange at the Pergamene market and addresses other legal issues related to "default, distraint, and trial." Hadrian sets both regulation and adjudication standards for Pergamene business transactions; here, imperial authority both intervenes in the minutiae of local markets and invokes imperial judicial frameworks for enforcement.[15] The letter largely focuses on complaints that Hadrian has received about money changers in the city:

[. . .] Ἡ(λ)έ(γ)χθησαν μετὰ τοῦτο καὶ ἕτερά τινα συνκεχω-
ρηκότες ἑαυτοῖς κερδῶν ὀνόματα ἀσπρατούραν τε καὶ τὸ
καλούμενην παρ᾽ αὐτοῖς προσφάγιον, δι᾽ ὧν ἐπηρέαζον μά-
λιστα τοὺς τὸν ἰχθὺν πιπράσκοντας.

Καὶ ταῦτα οὖν ἐδοκιμάσαμεν διορθῶσθαι· πλεονεκτεῖσθαι
γὰρ καὶ τοὺς ὀλίγους ὑπ᾽ αὐτῶν ἀνθρώπους (οὐ δίκ)αιον ἦν,
συνέβαινεν δὲ πᾶσιν αἰσθητὴν γείνεσθαι τοῖς ὠνουμένοις τὴν
ἄδικον τῶν πιπρασκόντων ζημίαν.

[. . .] After this it was proved that they had agreed on profits under certain other names, the kickbacks,[16] and the so-called fish-charge, with which they particularly harassed the fish-sellers.

Therefore, we decided that these things should be corrected; for it is not right that a few people should be defrauded by them, and it happened that all the purchasers were affected by the unjust loss applied to the vendors.[17]

It is expected that participants in markets (here money changers) should be able to exact some profit from exchanges, especially if they control the resources or hold a monopoly on the right to make that exchange. Money changers, Hadrian acknowledges, should largely be able to set the currency-exchange rates in Pergamon. Hadrian intervenes, however, because the money changers are setting different exchange rates for other vendors who are permitted to transact in nonlocal currency, bypassing the money changers. Fish sellers, who accept multiple forms of currency in their course of business, face extra markups when they go to money changers to convert currency. They complain that these markups cause them unjust loss. Hadrian reminds money changers that their profit margins cannot be set to such extremes as to cause unjust loss to other vendors. Those who control the currency exchanges in Pergamon are prohibited from creating unjust market conditions that disrupt other businesses.

While this second-century CE imperial letter does not directly parallel Philippians 3, this example demonstrates the regulatory context in which one might encounter the accounting language of gains and losses. Hadrian's more measured response also highlights the extremity of the theo-economic exchange Paul describes in Philippians 3. The extremity of this accounting system matches with the extremity of the rest of the chapter, in which Paul refers to "dogs" (*kuōn*) and "those who mutilate the flesh" (*katatomē*).[18] This terminology, coupled with the already mentioned devaluation of all things as *skubala* or "excrement," sets up Christ as a commodity that has an exclusive and valuable exchange rate set by Paul. By setting up the terms of exchange, Paul is in control of the exchange rates for Christ and status. Christ is the object for which Paul trades rather than the arbiter of exchange. Christ is the profit that Paul gains.

God-Profits in Antiquity

Before returning to an analysis of Phil 3:7–11 in order to explore the payoff of Paul's investment in the Christ-profit in Phil 3:10–11, it is worth pausing to answer some questions that arise from considering Christ as an object of investment. In what ways did people in antiquity describe the effect of the gods on profits and losses? Are the gods responsible for humanity's business, or are humans also responsible for the profits of the gods? After looking at a range of literary evidence, I will turn to Lucian's *Lives for Sale*, a text that takes the idea of divine-human exchange to a greater extreme by depicting humans and gods participating in a slave market.

Many texts argue that the gods actually determine the results of human efforts and control whether humans experience economic gains or losses. While human beings may attempt to control fate and bring about their own success, the gods are ultimately in control. The sixth-century BCE elegiac poet Theognis regularly makes this point. While early, Theognis has a strong and late manuscript tradition, including mention of his poetry in the Byzantine Suda. This text, presumably, would have also been available in the first century CE.[19]

Οὐδείς, Κύρν', ἄτης καὶ κέρδεος αἴτιος αὐτός,
ἀλλὰ θεοὶ τούτων δώτορες ἀμφοτέρων·
οὐδέ τις ἀνθρώπων ἐργάζεται ἐν φρεσὶν εἰδώς,
ἐς τέλος εἴτ' ἀγαθὸν γίνεται εἴτε κακόν.
πολλάκι γὰρ δοκέων θήσειν κακὸν ἐσθλὸν ἔθηκεν,
καί τε δοκῶν θήσειν ἐσθλὸν ἔθηκε κακόν.
οὐδέ τωι ἀνθρώπων παραγίνεται, ὅσσα θέλησιν·
ἴσχει γὰρ χαλεπῆς πείρατ' ἀμηχανίης.
ἄνθρωποι δὲ μάταια νομίζομεν εἰδότες οὐδέν·
θεοὶ δὲ κατὰ σφέτερον πάντα τελοῦσι νόον.

No one is themself the cause of loss and gain, Cyrnus;
But the gods are the givers of them both:
nor does any person work while knowing in their heart
whether it is toward a good end or a bad one.
For often, thinking to do a bad thing, one does a good thing,
And thinking to do a good thing, one does a bad thing.

And no person attains the things that they want;
For the limits of lack holds us back.
We humans consider in vain, knowing nothing
And the gods do everything according to their own
    judgment.[20]

Addressing his poem to his *erōmenos* Cyrnus, Theognis differentiates between intentions and outcomes; humans may work with the best of intentions, but it is the gods who ultimately control the outcome. Theognis observes that humans must labor ignorant of the future, and human intentions do not always match up with outcomes, including financial outcomes. Theognis offers a philosophical reflection on human intention and futility couched in financial terminology and makes the theological claim that all human gains and losses are sourced from the gods rather than from human effort. The gods control future outcomes for humans.

Hesiod, the eighth-century BCE poet offers a more complex description of divine involvement in human profits in the agrarian poem *Works and Days* (the most frequently cited text of Hesiod in the Roman period). While again quite early, Hesiod is frequently cited by authors of the first century CE, including Ovid, Lucian, and Quintilian.[21] In a land dispute with his brother Perses, Hesiod attempts to make the point that hard work is the proper source of wealth rather than bribing corrupt justices. To bolster his argument, Hesiod makes the point that the gods only grant long-term wealth and success to those who work justly, using several myths as examples of divine justice. After a long aside critiquing those judges who corruptly flout divine justice in pursuit of wealth, Hesiod returns to his main theme of proper work as the source of wealth.

χρήματα δ' οὐχ ἁρπακτά· θεόσδοτα πολλὸνἀμείνω. εἰ γάρ
τις καὶ χερσὶ βίῃ μέγαν ὄλβον ἕληται, ἠ' ὅ γ' ἀπὸ γλώσσης
ληίσσεται, οἷά τε πολλὰγίνεται, εὖτ' ἂν δὴ κέρδος νόον
ἐξαπατήσειἀνθρώπων, Αἰδῶ δέ τ' Ἀναιδείη κατοπάζῃ, ῥεῖα δέ
μιν μαυροῦσι θεοί, μινύθουσι δὲ οἶκον, ἀνέρι τῷ, παῦρον δέ τ'
ἐπὶ χρόνον ὄλβος ὀπηδεῖ.

Property is not to be snatched: god-given is better by far. For
if someone grabs great wealth with his hands by violence, or

plunders it by means of his tongue, as often happens when profit deceives the mind of human beings and shamelessness drives shame away, then the gods easily make him obscure, and they diminish that man's household, and wealth attends him for only a short time.[22]

This divine-human accounting system is more complex, because Hesiod acknowledges that humans can achieve gain (*kerdos*) in a variety of ways, both through their own work and through improper means. Wealth achieved from proper labor is understood as god-given (*theosdota*) and will lead to long-term success. When wealth is achieved through improper means, however, the gods will, over time, shrink those household profits. *Works and Days* contrasts wealth earned through an honest living, which for Hesiod includes land management and farming, and ill-gotten gains achieved through bribery, unjust legal decisions, and even violence. While humans do have some control over their own actions and outcomes, they can only avoid divine judgment for a little while. The only lasting wealth comes from the gods and from proper work (preferably as a gentleman farmer).

While these examples highlight the influence of the gods on human experiences of gain and loss, other texts take different perspectives. Greek tragedy often includes examples in which it is clear that the gods are dependent on humans for financial profit rather than the other way around. Euripides's *Philoctetes*, a tragedy preserved in fragment by later authors, contains one example.[23] An envoy from Troy addresses Philoctetes in an attempt to convince him to rejoin the Trojan War:

(ΠΡΕΣΒΥΣ ΤΡΩΣ)
ὁρᾶτε δ᾽ ὡς κἀν θεοῖσι κερδαίνειν καλόν, θαυμάζεται δ᾽ ὁ πλεῖστον ἐν ναοῖς ἔχωνχρυσόν· τί δῆτα καὶ σὲ κωλύει (λαβεῖν) κέρδος, παρόν γε, κἀξομοιοῦσθαι θεοῖς;

(Trojan ambassador)
You see that making a profit is honourable among the gods too, and that the one with most gold in his temples is admired! What prevents you too from (taking) profit, then, when it is quite possible, and from making yourself like the gods?[24]

While this passage is fragmentary and its broader context is uncertain, it is located at some point in a broader dialogue of the Trojans' attempts to encourage Philoctetes to rejoin the war efforts. The argument from this envoy encourages Philoctetes to return if for no other reason than to gain wealth and admiration from war spoils. The logic of this argument rests on a theological claim that gods make profits from human beings and receive admiration dependent on the amount of wealth they have stored up in their temples. Humans who make gains can become like the gods. Humans and gods alike seek wealth and admiration, and while unspoken, the clear implication is that the source of divine wealth that the gods keep in their temples comes from temple business. Temple business only happens through human interactions with the gods, including donations and sacrifices. Wealth and admiration are not distributed evenly among humans and gods, which means that enterprising humans can climb a divine-human wealth ladder and make themselves like the gods by becoming wealthy. Divine-human status itself seems tied up in resource control; the wealthiest humans are like the gods, while the poorest gods are like humans in their poverty.

A second example comes from fragments of Euripides's *Archelaus*, preserved in the Florilegium of Orion dating to the fifth century CE. This section is fragmentary, so it is unclear who is speaking, although it is probably the chorus.

> Ἐ[κ] τῶν δικαίων γὰρ νόμοι ταὐξήματα μεγάλα φέρουσιν,
> πάντα δ᾽ ἀνθρώποις (καλά). τάδ᾽ ἐστὶ χρήματ᾽, ἤν τις εὐσε-
> βῇ θεόν.

> Laws bring about great increase as a result of just actions, and thus make everything (good?) for mortals. This is genuine wealth: respect for god.

> Μακάριος ὅστις νοῦν ἔχων τιμᾷ θεὸν καὶ κέρδος αὑτῷ τοῦτο
> ποιεῖται μέγα.

> Happy is the one who has the good sense to honour god and to turn this to great profit for himself.[25]

This text interweaves systems of human profit with divine justice, and it commodifies respect for God (*eusebeia*) and honor (*timē*). *Timē*

also has a theo-economic sense to it, as it includes the sense of valuation and price as well as honor. The second saying plays with this
dual meaning. Those who have the proper valuation of the gods are
able to turn that price or honor to their personal gain. Humans are
able to leverage the gods; through proper orientation to the divine,
one is able to derive profit, even if the profit itself is *eusebeia*. When
paired, these two sayings make theo-economic claims: *eusebeia* is not
only theological but economic; respect for God is a form of wealth.
Timē is advantageous to both humans and the gods in a mutually
beneficial relationship that brings profit to both.[26]

Another system of divine-human loss and profit is the sacrificial system associated with cult. This topic frequently becomes
the butt of jokes for ancient comedists, including Menander. This
fourth-century BCE joke about human investment in sacrifice to
the gods is quoted in Athenaeus, a second- to third-century CE
rhetorician.

καὶ θύοντες μὲν τοῖς θεοῖς ὀλίγιστα εἰς τὰς θυσίας
καὶ τὰ τυχόντα δαπανῶμεν, ὥσπερ ὁ καλὸς Μένανδρος
ἐν τῇ Μέθῃ παρίστησιν
εἶτ᾽ οὐχ ὅμοια πράττομεν καὶ θύομεν·
ὅπου γε τοῖς θεοῖς μὲν ἠγορασμένον
δραχμῶν ἄγω προβάτιον ἀγαπητὸν δέκα, αὐλητρίδας δὲ καὶ
     μύρον καὶ ψαλτρίας,
Μενδαῖον, Θάσιον, ἐγχέλεις, τυρόν, μέλι
μικροῦ ταλάντου· γίνεται τὸ κατὰ λόγον
δραχμῶν μὲν ἀγαθὸν ἄξιον λαβεῖν δέκα
ἡμᾶς, ἐὰν καὶ καλλιερηθῇ τοῖς θεοῖς,
τούτων δὲ πρὸς ταῦτ᾽ ἀντανελεῖν τὴν ζημίαν.
πῶς οὐχὶ τὸ κακὸν τῶν ἱερῶν διπλάζεται;
ἐγὼ μὲν οὖν ὤν γε θεὸς οὐκ εἴασα τὴν
ὀσφὺν ἂν ἐπὶ τὸν βωμὸν ἐπιθεῖναί ποτε,
εἰ μὴ καθήγιζέν τις ἅμα τὴν ἔγχελυν,
ἵνα Καλλιμέδων ἀπέθανεν, εἷς τῶν συγγενῶν.

When we sacrifice to the gods, we spend as little as we can
     on the meal
and the incidentals, as the noble Menander
establishes in his drunkenness:

So doesn't how we do in life match the way we sacrifice?
Since I'm bringing the gods a nice little goat purchased for
    ten drachmas,
whereas the cost of the dancing-girls, perfume, harp-girls,
Mendaean and Thasian wine, eels, cheese, and honey
is minimal—a talent. And it's reasonable
for us to get ten drachmas worth of blessings—
assuming the gods take pleasure in the sacrifice!
But if we have to match what we spend on them with what
        we spend on ourselves, isn't the trouble sacrifices put us
        to doubled?
If I were a god, I'd never let anyone put the tailbone on the
        altar
unless he simultaneously offered his eel—
which would be the death of its relative Callimedon![27]

Although the joke here is that humans spend more on themselves on sacrificial banquets than on the banquets themselves, the humor is only legible because of its underlying logic: humans invest in the gods through sacrifice, and the gods derive benefit from sacrifice. Humans also expect a return on that investment in the form of divine favor; Menander is able to mock "the ten drachmas worth of blessings" as a critique of the larger sacrificial accounting system, in which humans try to set "prices" for certain divine benefits. The ancient sacrificial system that undergirds cult practice in antiquity is also a financial system. Menander describes a human-divine economy in which sacrificial transactions exchange sacrifice and devotion for divine favor. The most basic cultic interactions between divine and human are critiqued as quid pro quo transactions. The gods have an implicit price list for their theological favors, and humans can make choices about how to transact with the gods in ways that prove beneficial to them.

Lucian, the second-century CE satirist, is also fond of mocking the idea of theological favors. In an early passage in *On Sacrifices*, he argues that the gods only act when they receive sacrifice.[28]

Οὕτως οὐδέν, ὡς ἔοικεν, ἀμισθὶ ποιοῦσιν ὧν ποιοῦσιν, ἀλλὰ
πωλοῦσιν τοῖς ἀνθρώποις τἀγαθά, καὶ ἔνεστι πρίασθαι παρ᾽

αὐτῶν τὸ μὲν ὑγιαίνειν, εἰ τύχοι, βοϊδίου, τὸ δὲ πλουτεῖν βοῶν
τεττάρων, τὸ δὲ βασιλεύειν ἑκατόμβης, τὸ δὲ σῶον ἐπανελθεῖν
ἐξ Ἰλίου εἰς Πύλον ταύρων ἐννέα, καὶ τὸ ἐκ τῆς Αὐλίδος εἰς
Ἴλιον διαπλεῦσαι παρθένου βασιλικῆς. ἡ μὲν γὰρ Ἑκάβη τὸ
μὴ ἁλῶναι τὴν πόλιν τότε ἐπρίατο παρὰ τῆς Ἀθηνᾶς βοῶν
δώδεκα καὶ πέπλου. εἰκάζειν δὲ χρὴ πολλὰ εἶναι ἀλεκτρυόνος
καὶ στεφάνου καὶ λιβανωτοῦ μόνου παρ᾽ αὐτοῖς ὤνια.

So nothing, it seems, that they do is done without compensation. They sell men their blessings, and one can buy from
them health, it may be, for a calf, wealth for four oxen, a
royal throne for a hundred, a safe return from Troy to Pylos
for nine bulls, and a fair voyage from Aulis to Troy for a
king's daughter! Hecuba, you know, purchased temporary
immunity for Troy from Athena for twelve oxen and a frock.
One may imagine, too, that they have many things on sale
for the price of a cock or a wreath or nothing more than
incense.[29]

Lucian is even more explicit than Menander here in describing
a divine-human marketplace mediated through sacrifice. The divine will not act unless offered the properly calibrated sacrifice for
the blessing sought. Lucian critiques this entire sacrificial system,
but the argument for this critique rests on two points: first, humans think they can buy just about anything from the gods, and
second, the gods and their divine favors are cheaply bought. One
can purchase health for a calf, a safe voyage from Troy for a few
bulls, or cheaper blessings for even less. Lucian suggests that the
divine-human market exchange rate is dependent on both supply
and demand—humans and gods both have needs for divine favors,
on the one hand, and for dedicated offerings and sacrifices, on the
other.

The variety of literary evidence that uses language of *kerdos* and
zēmia to think about the gods demonstrates that there is no monolithic way in which persons in antiquity understood systems of profit
and loss vis-à-vis human-divine interactions. While some texts
understand human economic systems as under divine control or influence, others suggest that the gods are dependent on humanity for

their own cultic systems of profit and loss. What is clear, however, is that persons in antiquity frequently turned to financial language to think through their relationship with the divine. This suggests that a range of divine-human accounting systems lie within ancient theological imaginaries and that persons in antiquity use the language of profit and loss, the same language we find in Philippians 3, to describe their relationships with the divine. Persons in antiquity understand healing, divine favor, protection, honor, and piety, what we moderns might consider traditionally theological topics, as part of a larger contextual map in which theology and the economy were deeply entangled.

Commodified Divines

What does the divine-human accounting sheet of Phil 3:7–11 look like? In these verses, Paul does not turn to the language of sacrifice—although that language appears thrice in the letter. In Phil 2:17, Paul writes about being poured out as a drink offering and service for the faith of the Philippians. In Phil 3:3, Paul uses the language of temple service to describe those who serve in the spirit of God, and Phil 2:25 uses the language of *leitourgos* to describe Epaphroditus's work for Paul.[30] So, on the one hand, Paul and others understand their labor in service to God (which often does occur in a temple-sacrificial setting). However, the heart of the financial terminology in 3:7–11 and the divine-human exchange for Christ cannot be fully explained through the logic of the cultic system of sacrifice,[31] because in this exchange, Paul is acquiring Christ and profiting from that investment.

Some of our texts, particularly those on sacrifice, describe humanity's ability to buy off the gods, but none so far has addressed whether humanity can actually buy and sell divine figures. An example can be found, though, in Lucian's *Lives for Sale*. The setting of *Lives for Sale* is a divine-human slave market, overseen by Zeus and Hermes. Zeus and Hermes auction off slaves to a variety of buyers, and Hermes acts as the go-between for the transactions. Each slave who appears for sale is a famous philosopher, and each is questioned about their way of life, examined and commented on by the gods and their human buyers, and then sold to the highest bidder. The answers of the philosophers and their physical appearances match famous stories about them or reveal details about their school of philosophy. When Pythagoras comes up for sale, he is revealed as a divine or semidivine figure.[32]

ΑΓΟΡΑΣΤΗΣ: Καλῶς πάντα ἔφης καὶ ἱεροπρεπῶς. ἀλλὰ ἀπόδυθι, καὶ γυμνὸν γάρ σε ἰδεῖν βούλομαι. ὦ Ἡράκλεις, χρυσοῦς αὐτῷ ὁ μηρός ἐστι. θεός, οὐ βροτός τις εἶναι φαίνεται· ὥστε ὠνήσομαι πάντως αὐτόν. πόσου τοῦτον ἀποκηρύττεις;
ΕΡΜΗΣ: Δέκα μνῶν.
ΑΓΟΡΑΣΤΗΣ: Ἔχω τοσούτου λαβών.
ΖΕΥΣ: Γράφε τοῦ ὠνησαμένου τοὔνομα καὶ ὅθεν ἐστίν.
ΕΡΜΗΣ: Ἰταλιώτης, ὦ Ζεῦ, δοκεῖ τις εἶναι τῶν ἀμφὶ Κρότωνα καὶ Τάραντα καὶ τὴν ταύτῃ Ἑλλάδα· καίτοι οὐχ εἷς, ἀλλὰ τριακόσιοι σχεδὸν ἐώνηνται κατὰ κοινὸν αὐτόν.

BUYER: You have explained everything duly and sacerdotally. Come, strip, for I want to see you unclothed. Heracles! His thigh is of gold! He seems to be a god and not a mortal, so I shall certainly buy him. (to Hermes.) What price do you sell him for?
HERMES: Ten minas.
BUYER: I'll take him at that figure.
ZEUS: Write down the buyer's name and where he comes from.
HERMES: He appears to be an Italian, Zeus, one of those who live in the neighbourhood of Croton and Tarentum and the Greek settlements in that quarter of the world. But there is more than one buyer; about three hundred have bought him in shares.[33]

When the buyer, who is examining Pythagoras before sale, sees his golden thigh, he recognizes him as a god. Rather than stopping the auction, this news convinces the buyer that this is a smart purchase. Hermes offers Pythagoras for an incredibly cheap ten minas, and the buyer is revealed to represent an Italian *koinōn* (investment group) that has chosen to invest in Pythagoras. In this philosopher slave market, buyers are represented as followers of the philosophy, and the gods oversee the exchanges that occur in this divine-human market. Lucian makes the point that following a particular school of philosophy requires an investment by its followers. When the humans who choose to collectively organize themselves around a school of philosophy describe themselves as a *koinōn*, they signal mutual investment by using a cognate of the *koinōnia* that we have seen in the Letter to the Philippians. Lucian presents a marketplace in which gods and humans intermingle, using the language of slavery to depict human devotion to a particular way of life and to make claims about what and who is valued within a divine-human economy. Paul, in Philippians 3, is also mapping out the divine-human economy and imagining human devotion to a particular way of life. Lucian and Paul, too, use the language of slavery to describe human-divine entanglements.

The Benefits of the Christ-Profit and Christ in the Form of a Slave

Although gaining Christ and acquiring wealth in him require extreme devaluation of self (Phil 3:8), Paul thinks the exchange is a worthwhile investment. Paul writes in Phil 3:10–11 that he makes this transaction:

> τοῦ γνῶναι αὐτὸν καὶ τὴν δύναμιν τῆς ἀναστάσεως αὐτοῦ καὶ
> κοινωνίαν παθημάτων αὐτοῦ, συμμορφιζόμενος τῷ θανάτῳ
> αὐτοῦ, εἴ πως καταντήσω εἰς τὴν ἐξανάστασιν τὴν ἐκ νεκρῶν.

> in order to know [Christ] and the power of his resurrection
> and a share in his sufferings, being conformed to his death, if
> somehow I might attain resurrection from the dead.

Christ is not only the object in which Paul invests but also a partner in a *koinōnia* with Paul in sufferings. Paul invests in the suffering with Christ in order to be molded into Christ's death and ultimately to attain an inheritance of resurrection from the dead.

As we have seen in chapter 2, Julien Ogereau's work demonstrates that *koinōnia* expresses partnership, frequently occurring in business transactions.[34] In Philippians 1 and 4, Paul names a *koinōnia* with the Philippians in "the matter of giving and receiving" (Phil 4:15). In Phil 4:14, Paul acknowledges that the Philippians through their own giving are able to partner with him in suffering, and they can join Paul's suffering through the concern they show for him. Just as a group of Italians invest jointly in Pythagoras in Lucian's *Lives for Sale*, Paul invites the Philippians to have a share in the gospel and invest with him in suffering through their support. In Philippians 3, though, Paul presents himself as the sole partner in a *koinōnia* of suffering with Christ. This partnership offers the ultimate return on investment, but it also requires devaluing all for the acquisition of the Christ-profit. Here, Paul is the only one with direct access to the suffering *koinōnia* with Christ. While the Philippians also have access to partnership with Christ, it is mediated through Paul's *koinōnia* in suffering.

Feminist scholars such as Elizabeth Castelli, Cynthia Kittredge, and Joseph Marchal have long noted the prominence of language of unity and imitation throughout the letter and have demonstrated the ways in which this language reveals how power is negotiated among Paul and the Philippian assemblies. Paul attempts to assert a hierarchy in which he serves as the model for the Philippians,[35] using language related to *mimēsis* (imitation) and *phronein* (having a mind-set).[36] More recently, Marchal has noted the centrality of *koinōnia* and argued that it, too, might factor in the letter's larger themes of unity and imitation.[37] Marchal is right that *koinōnia* paired with rhetoric around unity and imitation attempts to reinforce hierarchy within the letter, but his analysis does not address the financial valences of *koinōnia* in this letter in which finances and imprisonment are as important to the occasion of the letter as unity and imitation are. By examining the *koinōnia* language throughout the letter but especially in its proximity to suffering, it becomes clear that Paul is not only trying to establish himself as a model for the Philippians through his imprisonment but also trying to remind them that he is their broker. Their partnership with him in the gospel is not, in his framing, an equal one.

In addition to partnering with Christ in suffering, Paul also hopes to be formed in Christ's death. In Phil 3:7–11, Paul offers two linguistic ties to other portions of the letter, raising the value of his contribution to the gospel. First, *kerdos* connects the divine-human exchange of Phil 3:7–11 with Phil 1:21, where Paul argues that living is Christ and dying is *kerdos*. Paul links his imprisonment to Christ's suffering; suffering is so valuable that it allows him to hope to attain resurrection from the dead. Second, *summorphizomenos* in Phil 3:10 connects with Phil 2:6–7, where Christ is described as existing in the *morphē* of God and taking on the *morphē* of a slave.[38] Paul's conformity with Christ's death echoes Christ's form as a slave; this logic is legible in the broader context of Phil 3:7–11 in which Christ is both a commodity and a partner in investment.[39] Paul's conformity with Christ's death is conformity into Christ's slavery, and Paul and Timothy claim at the outset of the letter to be slaves of Christ.

Paul's invocation of language of slavery occurs in a context in which slavery was ubiquitous and Christ-following communities included enslaved persons and slave owners in membership and leadership.[40] Significant scholarship exists on the language of slavery in the letters of Paul, which helps us to consider these realities in light of the language of slavery in Philippians. Dale Martin's book *Slavery as Salvation* contends that Paul and Christ-following communities mirrored elite literary tropes about slavery and status reversals, noting the ways in which certain slaves of the super-elite, when freed, were able to achieve significant wealth and status. While he largely focuses on the Corinthian correspondence and not Philippians, Martin argues that Philippians 2:6–11 "says that the closest analogy to what the gospel says of Christ's death and resurrection is the dramatic reversal in status of a slave whose obedience and unjust punishment are recompensed by an exaltation to a position of authority."[41] Other scholarship has made the important critique that leaning on elite tropes of playing with slavery as a metaphor elides the experience of enslaved persons whom Paul worked with and who would have perhaps carried, read, and, received his letters.[42] Lastly, it is important to note that despite that elision, enslaved persons were in cultic leadership in antiquity, including in early Christ-following communities.[43] Unlike Lucian's slave-market trope, written for an elite audience that would have encountered slave markets as buyers and not products, early Christ communities included a broader range of statuses and experiences with enslavement.

What is clear, though, is that the mixed metaphor of thinking of Christ both as an object of investment and in slave form is in fact quite legible, even when used to assign meaning and value to suffering. After all, slavery is simultaneously an economic system reliant on the buying and selling of human beings and an exploitative system reliant on violence, social death, and punishment.[44] "The acceptance of slavery as an ineradicable constituent of human society was strengthened rather than diminished by its universalization as metaphor for the human condition. . . . The belief that all human beings are slaves in the metaphysical sense . . . does not produce the effect of a social leveling."[45] Paul's use of language of enslavement is exploitative given his own free status, but the Philippian communities knew the complex realities and experiences of both slavery and freedom and also knew what it was to experience suffering and to support those who were suffering (cf. Phil 4:14; 2 Cor 8:2).[46] The entanglement of financial language and the imagery of slavery to describe suffering, value, and death might have been legible as an alternative theological and economic imaginary to those for whom such experiences were not an elite metaphor but lived reality.

Paul adds suffering and death to the tally sheet of divine accounting. By calculating his own imprisonment and the possibility of death (in Phil 1:21) with his partnership in Christ's suffering, Paul adds an additional exchange rate to a topsy-turvy divine price list in which gains are losses and losses are gains by arguing that his suffering is an investment and his death is a profit.

The Trust of Christ

Paul acquires wealth in Christ in Phil 3:9 in the form of righteousness from God that comes through faith in/of Christ (*dia pisteōs Christou*). It is not necessary (or possible) here to solve the objective/subjective genitive debate for *pistis Christou*.[47] Given the financial language in Phil 3:7–11, it is worth considering Teresa Morgan's *Roman Faith and Christian Faith: Pistis and Fides in the Early Roman*

Empire and Early Churches, which offers some alternatives to the en-
trenched positions over how to read *pistis Christou* in Gal 2:16, 20;
Gal 3:22; Rom 3:22, 26; and Phil 3:9. She asks, "What did the *pistis*
lexicon mean to early followers of Christ—to those who composed,
heard, or read the texts of the New Testament in the first century—
that made it so significant?"[48] Looking at a range of Greco-Roman
and Jewish literature as well as legal and epigraphic materials, she
reconsiders the linguistic range of *pistis*. Arguing against anachronistic readings of *pistis* and *fides* in New Testament and early Christian texts with a later Christian understanding of faith as related to
propositional beliefs, Morgan traces the history of the terms, noting
that the best way to understand these terms is as "trust/trustworthi-
ness." She explores the sense of *pistis* as the notion of giving credit
to something—in other words, that at its earliest stages, *pistis* is itself
a theological and economic term. Morgan's reading of *pistis* in Paul
is within a semantic range rooted in mutuality. Thus, *pistis* indicates
Christ's trust in God and trustworthiness to humanity as well as humanity's trust in Christ's trustworthiness.[49]

Given the earlier economic connotations of *pistis*, though, given
the importance of financial themes throughout Philippians, and
given the proximity of financial *termini technici*, why shift away from
the economic valences of *pistis* in Phil 3:9? Phil 3:9 clearly indicates
some degree of mutuality, but given its appearance in the context
of a divine-human transaction, why should it not retain some of its
financial connotations? The theo-economic valences of the terms
around Phil 3:9, however, make it difficult to read this instance of
pistis Christou in the way that Morgan, Peter Oakes, and John Barclay do for Galatians. The simpler reading in Philippians is to include Morgan's earlier definition of trust and credit. *Pistis Christou*
is the point of sale at which Paul (and the Philippians, if they follow
his example) transact with God to obtain righteousness by putting
credit in Christ. Paul advocates giving full trust in the Christ commodity, which pays off in righteousness that comes from God (Phil
3:9). Because of the inherent mutuality of *pistis*, the *pistis Christou* of
Philippians 3:9 also communicates the credit-worthiness of Christ.
Christ is a trustworthy and worthwhile investment that will pay off.
This is why Christ investment is so valuable that it is worth ex-
changing everything else of value.

Conclusion: An Economy of Suffering

The preponderance of theo-economic language throughout the Letter to the Philippians, especially concentrated in Philippians 2–3, contains terminology and concepts that are challenging and sometimes conflicted. At times Paul commodifies Christ, as in Phil 3:8. Elsewhere, Paul seems to be the sole partner in suffering with Christ, as in Phil 3:10–11. These images nonetheless build to demonstrate how Paul sets himself up as a broker in the gospel to the Philippians, offering them the Christ commodity, while also distancing their access to Christ by reminding them of his sole partnership with Christ in suffering. The Philippians' access to Christ through suffering comes through Paul's partnership with Christ.

Paul sets up a commodities exchange in which only he has the proper status to acquire Christ. Gaining the Christ-profit allows Paul not only to be the sole partner in a venture (*koinōnia*) of suffering (Phil 3:10) but also to attain to resurrection from the dead (Phil 3:11). There are theo-economic ties in between the valuation of suffering and the commodification of Christ in Philippians 3 and evocations of slavery and labor found in Philippians 2.

In many ways, the divine accounting system Paul offers in Phil 3:7–11 represents an alternative economy to the world of business transactions from which it draws its terminology. This is a system in which traditional sources of status and profits are upended, devalued in order to gain something of greater theological value, namely, Christ. This upending creates an economy of suffering in which human and divine suffering is assigned a value. This divine accounting system describes a venture in suffering that is worth investment, even if it means death, because it offers access to the benefit of resurrection from the dead. However, by sharing in suffering and thus in the larger venture with Christ, Paul sets himself up as the broker between God and the Philippians. He offers the Philippians an opportunity to share the risk and reward of the gospel, but only he has direct access (through his own suffering and imprisonment) to suffering with Christ. Because of the high price Paul sets for the Christ commodity and because of his sole access to the *koinōnia* of Christ's suffering, Paul is rhetorically the only one who mediates access to Christ. Despite being in (what would seem to be) the rhetorically disadvantageous place of being in prison and relying on the Philippians for community support, this alternative divine accounting system, laid out in Phil 3:7–11, means that Paul stands in the main contributing role. Nevertheless, in the theological price setting of Phil 3, a community that was familiar with suffering and hardship might have found their own experiences and status to be valuable in ways that might have been devalued in society.

CHAPTER FOUR

The Down Payment
of Righteousness

And can it be that I should gain
An interest in the Savior's blood?

—CHARLES WESLEY, "AND CAN IT BE?"

Theo-Economic Afterlives

WHAT IS THE AFTERLIFE of some of the theo-economic language in the Letter to the Philippians? What do other early Christian writers make of the blurring of divine-human financial exchange offered in the commodification of Christ in Philippians 3 or the security and venture language found in Philippians 1? In what ways is the economy of suffering outlined in the Letter to the Philippians put to use in other early Christian texts? How do other early Christian writers describe Christ as an object that can be bought, sold, traded, or otherwise used in divine-human transactions?

In this chapter, I take up these questions by turning to a letter or set of letters written some fifty to seventy-five years after Paul, partially preserved in Greek, Latin, and Syriac: Polycarp's *Letter to the Philippians* (Pol. *Phil.*).[1] In addition to the composite nature of the text and limited manuscript tradition, some of the themes of the letter have struck scholars and interpreters as disjointed. Along with identifying the forwarding of Ignatius's correspondence as an occasion for the letter, Polycarp addresses numerous other topics. These include a situation surrounding a former presbyter named Valens, who, along with his wife, "had engaged in some shady dealings, possibly involving the church's finances,"[2] as well as polemical concerns over teachings proliferating in the communities about the full humanity of Christ, resurrection, and future judgment.[3] The majority of the letter is spent in interpretation of a wide set of texts ranging from the letters of Paul (including the Pastoral Epistles), 1 Peter, Tobit, and sayings of Jesus from the gospels, coupled with teachings about "righteousness" offered, Polycarp claims, at the request of the Philippians.[4]

By focusing on Polycarp's use of some of the same theo-economic themes we found in Paul's letter to Philippi decades earlier, it becomes clear that these topics are less disjointed than at first glance. There are important theo-economic ties between this letter's focus on the use and misuse of money, exegesis of texts such as 1 Tim 6:10 ("for the love of money is the root of all evil"), concerns over false teaching, and emphasis on God's judgment. As Laura Nasrallah has recently put it, "In the second-century Philippian community in Christ, we find that issues of money—the dangerous love of money, and how benefaction can be liberative—still persist."[5] These issues of money, however, and the theo-economic rhetoric in which they are framed, unfurl in different directions from those found in Paul's Letter to the Philippians, even as they echo some of its same themes.

As a starting point for considering these themes, I focus on Pol. *Phil* 8.1–2, where Polycarp introduces the idea that Christ is the "down payment for our righteousness." We find that Polycarp understands both the use of money and following proper teaching within a juridical theo-economic context in which Christ has spent blood in suffering as a down payment for humanity's future judgment and that both right belief and right action are required in order to avoid being held liable for that down payment. This text expands the economy of suffering that we find in Paul's letter, where Christ and suffering are commodified. The commodification has been turned to marshal polemical ends and to attempt to regulate ecclesiastical structures.

It is important to acknowledge at the outset that there are potential difficulties in dating this text to the early second century. Some of these difficulties arise from the text itself; there is a discrepancy between the letter's ninth and thirteenth chapters, which makes relative chronological placement difficult. In chapter 9, Polycarp writes that Ignatius has already been martyred, while in chapter 13, Polycarp asks the Philippians to let him know what they "have learned more definitely about Ignatius himself and those who are with him" (Pol. *Phil.* 13.2), implying that Polycarp is unaware of Ignatius's ultimate fate. Chapter 13 also mentions Polycarp forwarding a collection of letters from Ignatius at the Philippians' request, appended to Polycarp's letter. The Philippians

ἐξ ὧν μεγάλα ὠφεληθῆναι δυνήσεσθε. περιέχουσι γὰρ πίστιν καὶ ὑπομονὴν καὶ πᾶσαν οἰκοδομὴν τὴν εἰς τὸν κύριον ἡμῶν ἀνήκουσαν.

will be able to profit greatly from them, for they deal with faith and endurance and all edification that is suitable in our Lord.[6]

Here, the letter form itself has become profitable for communities in Christ.

While a variety of explanations have been offered for this discrepancy, N. P. Harrison's argument that this letter is a compilation of at least two texts written perhaps some twenty-five years apart has become the dominant theory.[7] Another difficulty comes from the letter's ties to the Ignatian corpus, whose date and "authenticity," in its various recensions, is under continuous debate.[8] Because Polycarp has been used to argue in favor of earlier dating for the Ignatian materials, Polycarp is therefore also potentially suspect. This connection with Ignatius, along with the poor manuscript tradition, has led some scholars to reject various interpolation theories, although the second-century dating has largely remained intact despite its connection to Ignatius.[9]

While these questions are important, they do not immediately affect the focus of this chapter: an exploration of Polycarp's theo-economic language and of the ways in which Polycarp takes several phrases and themes from Philippians, particularly the com-modification of Christ, in a new direction. Polycarp makes use of Paul's concept of the commodification of Christ to serve his own letter's themes of divine judgment, right teaching and practice, and warnings against *philarguria* (love of money). Polycarp's letter fits as an example of early Christian writings that explicitly identify tradi-tions about cities with an apostolic connection via correspondence and then lay claim to those traditions. Polycarp, like other early Christian writers, fits his own teachings and theology into those traditions. In examining the theo-economic language that Poly-carp deploys, I am not arguing that the early Christ communities of Philippi had generations of money troubles but rather that Philippi's reputation as a city that received correspondence from Paul, as well as Philippians' preponderance of theo-economic language, led to a tradition of referencing Paul, the Philippians, and the first-century correspondence they exchanged to create further theo-economic interpretations.[10]

Christ as the Down Payment for Sin

In Pol. *Phil.* 2, Polycarp encourages the Philippians:

> δουλεύσατε τῷ θεῷ ἐν φόβῳ καὶ ἀληθείᾳ, ἀπολιπόντες
> τὴν κενὴν ματαιολογίαν καὶ τὴν τῶν πολλῶν πλάνην . . .
> ᾧ ὑπετάγη τὰ πάντα ἐπουράνια καὶ ἐπίγεια, ᾧ πᾶσα πνοὴ
> λατρεύσει, ὃς ἔρχεται κριτὴς ζώντων καὶ νεκρῶν, οὗ τὸ αἷμα
> ἐκζητήσει ὁ θεὸς ἀπὸ τῶν ἀπειθούντων αὐτῷ.

> You should slave for God in fear and truth, abandoning fu-tile reasoning and the error of many. . . . To him [Jesus] all things on heaven and on earth are subject, whom all breath-ing things serve, who will come in judgment of the living and the dead, and God will hold accountable those who dis-obey him for his blood.[11]

Echoing Phil 2:10–11 and 3:21 as well as 1 Cor 15:28, Polycarp emphasizes Christ's future judgment of the living and the dead, a judgment in which God is the one who will arbitrate accountability for Christ's blood. The outset of the letter intertwines a polemical concern with a reminder of future divine judgment. David Downs has noted that while avarice and heresy have "not often been understood in relation to one another," they "are closely connected in the logical progression of Polycarp's letter."[12] Eschatology is here described in a juridical context, and God is described as the one who demands an account for Christ's blood. It is hardly unusual to use a juridical setting to discuss accountability for the blood of prophets and innocent people.[13] But Polycarp expands this into cosmic terms, in which all beings are subject to a trial in which their slaving for God is weighed against Christ's blood.

In introducing future divine judgment and sin together, Polycarp offers an argument that is not atypical in both Second Temple Judaism and early Christianity.[14] The imagery used, here, is unusual because it describes Christ's death as a down payment for future judgment. Unlike other texts that use debt language to claim that Christ cancels humanity's indebtedness to sin[15] or repays it in full through the Passion,[16] this letter argues that both Polycarp and the Philippians should

> Ἀδιαλείπτως οὖν προσκαρτερῶμεν τῇ ἐλπίδι ἡμῶν καὶ τῷ ἀρραβῶνι τῆς δικαιοσύνης ἡμῶν, ὅς ἐστι Χριστὸς Ἰησοῦς, ὃς ἀνήνεγκεν ἡμῶν τὰς ἁμαρτίας τῷ ἰδίῳ σώματι ἐπὶ τὸ ξύλον.

> persevere, unremitting in our hope and in the down payment of our righteousness, which is Christ Jesus, who bore our sins in his own body upon the tree.[17]

Humanity has been given a down payment for righteousness, and their sins are borne upon Christ's body. Humanity will be called to account for their sins and for this down payment in future judgment.

This idea continues the theo-economic logic of Philippians 3, which I explored in chapter 3. Christ is a commodity[18] that is given a set value and then exchanged (Phil 3:7–11). In Philippians 3, Paul is willing to exchange all of his statuses for the Christ commodity in order to be in a venture (*koinōnia*) in suffering with him and attain resurrection from the dead. By representing Christ's status as a slave who died on the cross, Paul renders the image of the suffering Christ-body as a commodity that can be traded and in which he can invest, through his own conforming to that suffering. For Polycarp, that suffering Christ-body on the cross is now a commodity that has the value level of a down payment for humanity's sins. This theo-economic logic is intertwined with Polycarp's description of sin as obligation. This is also a juridical context, in which Christ both sits in judgment and weighs humanity's beliefs and actions alongside the down payment of the suffering Christ commodity.

What are the theological implications of an understanding of Christ as the down payment for righteousness? First, it is helpful to note that the language of *arrabōn*, down payment, is common language in contracts and other purchase agreements.[19] *Arrabōn* were given in contracts in which both parties had obligations. An *arrabōn* is a deposit made of money or an in-kind object, a security or pledge offered as an advance of further payment, and it is subject to forfeiture if the rest of the contract or payment is not fulfilled.[20]

Three examples of the use of this term in contracts indicate a consistent use of the idea of a down payment over several centuries. One example comes from a second-century CE fragmentary letter detailing a request for wine and vegetable seeds:

> χαίροις Ἥρων. εὐθέως
> πέμψον μοι ἐν ἀσκοῖς
> ἐκ τοῦ Ἀπολλῶ ἀπὸ τῆς ἀπο-
> θήκ(ης) ὀμφακίν(ου) μετ(ρητὰς) ε, ἐπὶ
> εἴληφα ἀρραβῶνα πρὸς (δραχμὰς) ρκ,
> καὶ λαχαν( ) (ἀρτάβας) η πρὸς (δραχμὰς) κε.
> παραχρῆμ(α) [. . .]
> ηση [. . .]
> δε [. . .]

> Greetings, Heron. Send me immediately in skins from the store in the house of Apollos 5 metretai of wine made from unripe grapes (?), since I have accepted a pledge for 120 drachmae, and 8 artabas of vegetable-seed (?) at 25 drachmae.[21]

In this letter, an unnamed sender writes to Heron, requesting that he immediately send along goods from Apollos's storehouse. The writer has accepted an *arrabōn* for those goods, and the writer now dashes off a quick note to Heron to provide the wine and seed so that the purchase can be completed. Here a down payment, as part of a larger sum owed within a transaction, begins a process of mail, labor, and transport that all constitute a larger transaction with larger sums at stake.

Perhaps a century later, a shipbuilding contract details how an *arrabōn* for the construction of a boat will be used. This labor contract (P.Mich.inv. 1972) is recorded on papyrus and is dated to 249 CE:

χοντ() πρὸς τ [. . .]
ἐμοῦ δὲ παρέχο[ντος . . .]
πηγου καὶ λεμβ [. . .]
στηση α [. . .] α [. . .]
δώδεκα καὶ δ [. . . ἑκά-]
στῳ δὲ τῶν ε [. . .]
ὀκτὼ καὶ ὑπὲ[ρ . . .]
καὶ ἐκτάκτων ναυπ[ηγῶν . . .]
α καὶ ἑκάστῳ ναυπη[γῶ δώσω κατὰ μῆνα πυ-]
ροῦ ἀρτάβην μίαν κ[αὶ . . . ἑκά-]
στῳ κατὰ μηνα χοίνι[κα(ς) . . .]
ὡς ἑκάστ(ῳ) κατὰ μῆν[α δοθήσεται ἐλαίου]
χρηστ(οῦ) κοτύλ(η) μία καὶ ξ [. . .]
χρόνου κεράμιον ἓν [καὶ ὁμολογῶ ἐσχη-]
κέναι εἰς ἀραβῶνος λόγ[ον δραχμὰς . . .]
αἵπερ κατὰ μέρος ἐ[ξοδιασθήσονται ὑπὲρ ἡ-]
μερησίων μισθ(ῶν). ἀρξόμε[νος δὲ ἀπὸ τοῦ ἐνεστῶ-]
τος μηνὸς Ἀθὺρ τοῦ ἐνε[στῶτος α (ἔτους) σοι ἐργά-]
σομαι μέχρις οὗ συντελίω[σις γένηται καὶ παρα-]
δώσω τὸ πλοῖον εὐάρεσ[τον καὶ καλὸν ἄνευ]
πάσης μέμψεως τέχνη[ς, οὔσης σοι τῆς πρά-]
ξεως παρά τε ἐμοῦ καὶ τῶν [ὑπαρχόντων μοι πάν-]
των. ἡ ἐπιδοχ(ὴ) κυρία κ[αὶ ἐπερωτηθ(εὶς) ὡμολ(όγησα).]
(ἔτους) α Αὐτοκράτορος Καίσ[αρος Γαίου Μεσσίου
    Κουίντου]
Δεκίου Τραιανοῦ Εὐσεβ[ο]ῦς Ε[ὐτυχοῦς Σεβαστοῦ]
Ἀθὺρ ιθ. Αὐρ(ήλιος) Ἡρᾶς Διογᾶτ[ος ἐπεδεξάμην τὴν κα-]

τασκευὴν τοῦ προκειμ[ένου πλοίου καὶ ἔσχηκα]
ἱς λόγον [το]ῦ ἀραβῶνος δραχ[μὰς . . . καὶ μισθὸν δώσω
    καθ᾽ ἕ-]
καστο[ν μ]ῆνα καὶ παρα[δώσω τὸ πλοῖον καθὼς]
πρόκ[ειται] καὶ ἐπερω[τηθ(εὶς) ὡμολόγησα.]

[. . .] And I shall give each shipbuilder monthly one artaba of wheat and [. . .] each one monthly x choichix (-kes) of [. . .] each one will be given monthly one kotyle of good olive oil and [. . .] period one keramion and I acknowledge that I have received as an *arrabōn* x drachmas that will be spent in part for daily wages. Starting from the present month Hathyr of the present 1st year I shall start to work for you until a discharge of obligations in full is reached and I shall hand over the boat in acceptable and good condition without any technical blame while you have the right of execution upon me and upon all my possessions. The lease is in effect and in answer to the formal question I gave my consent. Year 1 of Imperator Caesar Gaeus Messius Quintus Decius Trajanus Pius Felix Augustus, Hathyr 19. I, Aurelius Heras, son of Diogas, have taken upon me to build the aforementioned boat and I have received as an *arrabōn* x drachmas and I shall provide pay each month and I shall hand the boat over as written above and in answer to the formal questions I gave my consent.[22]

The verso of this fragmentary papyrus is sufficiently clear to understand that Aurelius Heras has agreed to build a boat and received a down payment (*arrabōn*) to fund the beginning of construction. While a lacuna obscures the amount of the down payment, the extant text clearly specifies how the earnest money will be used. Aurelius Heras, as the general contractor, explains to the buyer the wages he will offer, as well as wheat and olive oil in payment to each subcontractor. By specifying the amount each shipbuilder will receive, Heras offers the details of a labor contract in which ongoing work requires ongoing funding, but he also justifies the amount of the *arrabōn* by detailing how it will be spent. The down payment that Heras receives provides enough start-up funds for work on the project to begin, but if Heras fails to deliver on the promised boat, this contract stipulates that he and all of his possessions are on the line. An *arrabōn* is one way to begin funding production on a longer-term investment that might otherwise be out of financial reach, such as a boat.

What does Polycarp's description of Christ as *arrabōn* have to do with the larger context of judgment in the letter? Down payments also have a place within the juridical system. The following is a rescript,[23] a response from a proconsul to the city of Kos concerning the city's petition to the emperor Claudius in the mid-first century CE:

[Γν. Δομ]ίτιος Κορβούλων ἀνθύπατος
[Κῴω]ν ἄρχουσι βουλῇ δήμωι
χαίρειν
[Οὐκ ἀλυσιτε]λὲς ἡγησάμην πολλάκις
[καὶ πόλεσ]ι παραστῆσαι, ὅσα ἐν ἐμοὶ μά-
[λιστα, ὅτι ἃ] ἄξια δύναται νομίζεσθαι
[κρίσεω]ς εἶναι θείας τοῦ Σεβαστοῦ,
[πρότερον πρὸ]ς τοὺς ἐπὶ τῶν ἐπαρχει-
[ῶν πέμπεσθαι ἐν ταῖ]ς ἐντολαῖς ἐπι-
[τέτακται. νῦν δ᾽ ἐξ ὑμετ]έρου ψηφίσμα-
[τος ὁ δεῖνα ἐπίκ]λησιν ἔθετο ἐπὶ
[τὸν Σεβαστόν, καὶ ἦσ] θόμην ἐπηρείας
[ἔργο]ν αὐτὸν [τοῦ]το πεποιηκέναι. δε-
[ήσει τ]οίνυν, εἰ μὲν ἐπὶ τὸν Σεβαστὸν
[ἡ ἐπί] κλησις
γείνεται, πρότ[ε]ρον ἐμὲ
[ἐξετ]άσαι τὴν αἰτίαν, εἰ δὲ ἐπ᾽ ἐμέ, τὸ[ν]
[ταμία]ν ἀξιόχρεως λαβεῖν τοὺς ἀρρα-
βῶν]ας δηναρίων δισχειλίων πεν[τα]-
[κο]σίων κατὰ τὸ προτεθὲν ὑπ᾽ ἐμοῦ δι-
[άταγ]μα διὰ τοὺς φυγοδικοῦντας.
[ἐὰν δ]ὲ
πρὸς ταῦτα μὴ γε[ίνηται . . .][24]

[Gnaeus Dom]itius Corbulon proconsul to archons, council, demos [of the Koans], greetings. I have often considered it [useful] to remind [even cities], in respect to as many matters certainly as lie in my jurisdiction, that it has been ordered in the mandata that [whatever] matters are thought to be worthy of the sacred [decision] of the emperor [are first sent to] the provincial authorities. [So-and-so has just now] filed an application to [the emperor on the basis of] a decree of yours, [and] I perceived that he had done so in contempt (of the rule). Well then, it [will be] necessary that I first examine the reason; but if (it comes at all) to me, the [quaestor] must receive the *arrabōn* a value of 2,500 denarii according to the edict promulgated by me on account of the people who do not show up for trial. [If] he does not meet these requirements . . .[25]

Applicants from Kos have filed an appeal to the emperor without first going through the proper regional authority, and they have now received a rejoinder from the proconsul Corbulon. He reminds them that matters referred to the sacred judgment of the emperor must go through the proper channels, namely Corbulon.[26] Because Corbulon has many petitioners who skip out on their appeal date, he lets the applicants from Kos know that he requires a down payment of twenty-five hundred denarii before he will hear their appeal and consider passing it along to the emperor. This is to uphold an edict from the emperor requiring such a down payment in response to persons not appearing to offer a defense at trial. The appeal for sacred judgment, then, requires a demonstration that the Koans have the financing to follow through with their appeal and have enough on hand to pay for their defense.[27] Corbulon acts as a divine intermediary for the imperial sacred judgment, and he serves as gatekeeper for their access to the emperor. He is responsible for ensuring that they are prepared and have enough financing on hand to make their case when they get their day in court. Even as a free city, Kos still has to go through the proper bureaucratic channels and must meet certain financial obligations to be able to access divine justice.

Juridical contexts are the site of theo-economic thinking, especially within the context of the empire. This proto-rescript demonstrates that an appeal for imperial judgment includes theological elements, including the image of the emperor as the source of divine judgment. Humans with authority in the political-legal bureaucracy mediate human access to divine judgment, including requiring a down payment toward future judgment. This rescript also demonstrates that the imperial judicial system is also an economic system. Courts settle financial disputes, enforce contracts, and authorize debt collection. In addition, the very adjudication process requires bureaucracy, including financial bureaucracy, to function. Corbulon's insistence on a large down payment demonstrates that appeals for judgment require a significant investment of resources, not only for mounting a legal argument but even just to demonstrate that one has the financial ability to mount a legal argument. Access to justice requires significant wealth.

Obtaining justice is not only expensive but risky. Evidence from Gaius's *Institutes* describes many of the laws and cases that concern contracts, property disputes, and other legal matters with financial implications in which a judge is asked to require an action. In this second-century CE legal compendium, many cases require an initial payment from parties who are seeking legal judgment, which is then forfeited if one loses their case. To take a single example, Gaius mentions the *sacramentum*, "so called from the wager or forfeit, which involved the deposit by the parties in the hands of the Pontiffs, for the benefit of the *sacra publica*."[28] Both parties would swear an oath (the *sacramentum*), and the losing party not only would be obligated to settle whatever financial obligation the judgment required (often payment of a debt) but would also lose the money deposited to the *sacra publica* as a penalty for offering false testimony (taking a false oath). According to second-century CE legal writings, many legal proceedings require an initial payment before judgment can be rendered. These payments are used to demonstrate the ability of a person to meet the financial obligations of the case and to deter false testimony. A person who offered improper testimony when called to court could face drastic legal and financial consequences.

The shipbuilding contracts, rescript, and case law help us to untangle some of the theo-economic logic of Christ on the cross as the *arrabōn* for sin, and they help us to explain what language of down payment is doing in a text whose primary concern seems to be cosmic judgment. For Polycarp, Christ's suffering is the down payment on righteousness for an impending judgment of Christ, overseen by God, of sins. If the Philippians are unable to succeed in court, they risk the loss of that down payment and could be held liable for Christ's blood.

Paul as Warranty in Faith

How will the Philippians be prepared to render an account before God? Polycarp offers his own letter alongside the letter that the Philippians already have from Paul as guidance. Although Polycarp only once directly cites Paul's Letter to the Philippians,[29] thematic and linguistic themes from Paul echo throughout Polycarp's letter. These echoes often arise when Polycarp mentions those persons whom the Philippians should admire, especially Paul. In greeting, for example, Polycarp praises the community for having "received the replicas of true love" and "sent ahead those who were confined in chains fitting for saints."[30] This both continues the praise to the Philippians for having received a letter from Paul and also communicates that these later generations are continuing to live out themes that were important in that first communication, namely, imitation of proper models and care for people in chains.[31] Cognates of *mimēsis* feature prominently in both texts. Paul exhorts the Philippians to join in imitating him and those who live according to his example (Phil 3:17); Polycarp regularly references the examples that the Philippians have in Paul and others, and ultimately in Christ.[32] Thus, Polycarp tries to marshal authority for his own arguments by intertwining his letter with Paul's letter, thus tying his authority and example to the authority and examples they already have in Paul and in Christ.

Polycarp also rejoices because the Philippians have "the secure root [*hē bebaia*] of [their] faith, proclaimed from ancient times, [which] even now continues to abide and bear fruit in our Lord Jesus Christ."[33] This borrows the language Paul and Timothy use for the Philippians in Philippians 1, when praying that they will abound in the fruit of righteousness that is through Jesus Christ to the glory and praise of God (Phil 1:11). It also echoes the language that Paul uses for his imprisonment as a warranty (*bebaios*) for the gospel venture. Polycarp echoes theo-economic rhetoric already used by Paul for the Philippians as a divine agricultural worksite. Surveying the state of the Philippian fields decades letter, Polycarp is pleased with the deep roots of faith that support the Philippians' continued fruit bearing. These roots of the gospel were warrantied by Paul through his imprisonment. Thus, Paul is the warranty in both letters. Polycarp can invoke Paul's authority to bolster his own authority at the outset of the letter. For Polycarp, the fact that the Philippians are still bearing fruit generations later affirms that Paul's warranty of the gospel through his imprisonment has had lasting effect; these later generations too can have a share in Paul's joy (Phil 1:7).

Polycarp also makes much of the fact that the Philippians were the recipients of a letter from Paul, using this fact to shore up his own theme of righteousness throughout the letter:

οὔτε γὰρ ἐγὼ οὔτε ἄλλος ὅμοιος ἐμοὶ δύναται κατακολουθῆσαι τῇ σοφίᾳ τοῦ μακαρίου καὶ ἐνδόξου Παύλου, ὃς γενόμενος ἐν ὑμῖν κατὰ πρόσωπον τῶν τότε ἀνθρώπων ἐδίδαξεν ἀκριβῶς καὶ βεβαίως τὸν περὶ ἀληθείας λόγον, ὃς καὶ ἀπὼν ὑμῖν ἔγραψεν ἐπιστολάς, εἰς ἃς ἐὰν ἐγκύπτητε, δυνηθήσεσθε οἰκοδομεῖσθαι εἰς τὴν δοθεῖσαν ὑμῖν πίστιν.

For neither I nor anyone like me is able to replicate the wisdom of the blessed and glorious Paul. When he was with you he accurately and reliably taught the word of truth to those who were there at the time. And when he was absent he wrote you letters. If you carefully peer into them, you will be able to be built up in the faith that was given you.[34]

If the Philippians follow the model they have in Paul and other saints-in-chains, as well as the teachings offered to them in the letters received and remembered, they have a secure root of faith that will continue to bear fruit, and they will be built up in that faith. These later generations (and Polycarp) have Paul as their guide, and the faith received from Paul and his letter as their "mother."[35] By writing to the Philippians and additionally invoking Ignatius as a letter writer, Polycarp places himself in a line of letter writers who provide texts that can be studied for the edification of the community in faith. Their continued growth in faith is dependent on their following the models they already have. This potential also comes with a warning: the Philippians are at risk of not following Paul's example, whether by succumbing to love of money (*philarguria*),[36] by not agreeing with proper thinking concerning Christ and judgment,[37] or by following idle speculation from the multitudes and false teachings.[38]

Many of the warnings about false teachings, exhortations to righteousness, and instructions about the right conduct of various persons in the church focus on money. The first exhortation begins a run through proper conduct for widows, deacons, and others at the heart of the letter. This exhortation is a doubled quotation from 1 Timothy, including 1 Tim 6:10 ("For the love of money is the root of all evil") and 1 Tim 6:7 ("For we brought nothing into the world, and we can take nothing from it"). Widows, deacons, and presbyters are cautioned not to be lovers of money (*aphilarguroi*),[39] and all are encouraged to give alms, because "alms deliver from death" (*quia eleemosyna de morte liberat*).[40]

Polycarp also criticizes a former presbyter named Valens, who "misunderstand[s] the office that was given to him" (*sic ignoret is locum, qui datus est ei*).[41] Polycarp argues that one who cannot control himself cannot preach about self-control,[42] and it seems as though Valens's lack of self-control has something to do with financial matters. Polycarp tells the Philippians that "anyone who cannot avoid the love of money will be defiled by idolatry and will be judged as if among the outsiders who know nothing about the judgment of the Lord" (*si quis non se abstinuerit ab avaritia, ab idolatria coinquinabitur et tamquam inter gentes iudicabitur, qui ignorant iudicium domini*).[43] Here, also, Polycarp returns to his reminder that the Philippians have a special place among the churches because of their relationship with Paul: "But I have neither perceived nor heard that you have any such thing in your midst, among whom the most fortunate Paul labored and who are found in the beginning of his epistle" (*ego autem nihil tale sensi in vobis vel audivi, in quibus laboravit beatus Paulus, qui estis in principio epistulae eius*).[44] The Philippians, because they are ones among whom the blessed Paul worked, are able to keep themselves from love of money and other sins as long as they remember their place as the descendants of those who knew Paul working among them.

The Rewards and Penalties of a Cosmic Court

These financial instructions, which are tied to the warranty the Philippians have from Paul, are also tied to the cosmic juridical setting. The passage that immediately follows a set of instructions to presbyters, including a requirement to avoid *philarguria* (love of money), concludes a series of instructions for various members within the community:

> ἀπέναντι γὰρ τῶν τοῦ κυρίου καὶ θεοῦ ἐσμὲν ὀφθαλμῶν, καὶ πάντας δεῖ παραστῆναι τῷ βήματι τοῦ Χριστοῦ καὶ ἕκαστον ὑπὲρ αὐτοῦ λόγον δοῦναι.

> For we are before the eyes of the Lord and of God, and everyone must appear before the judgment seat of Christ, each rendering an account of him- or herself.[45]

The image of persons appearing to offer testimony or render their account before the *bēma* (judgment seat) of Christ frames the previous instructions within a cosmic juridical setting. The accounting Polycarp expects not only includes one's right practices (such as avoiding *philarguria*) but also includes a reckoning for one's agreement with right teaching. Polycarp seeks to control definitions of what right Christian thought and practice are, and he uses theo-economic language to make his polemical case.

Humanity follows through on Christ's down payment by means of right behavior and belief, according to Polycarp. This is how humanity "pays off" the outstanding balance left over from Christ's blood and offers a convincing witness before God. Christ's down payment represents an initial demonstration of humanity's ability to mount a defense at judgment, but it is up to the Philippians to follow through on this initial offering and help tip the scales in the right direction. The potential reward is immense. Polycarp reminds the Philippians,

> καὶ ὅτι ἐὰν πολιτευσώμεθα ἀξίως αὐτοῦ, καὶ συμβασιλεύσομεν αὐτῷ, εἴγε πιστεύομεν

> If we administer ourselves worthily of him, we would also rule together with him—so long as we trust.[46]

The Philippians, if they put their credit—the verb used is *pisteuo-men*[47]—in the right place, will be judged as worthy. Conversely, if they pursue the wrong direction or act unworthily, the Philippians will be held responsible not only for their own actions and beliefs but for the blood of Christ. They also will have damaged Paul's warranty. The Philippians are at risk of losing the down payment offered by Christ if they are unable to follow through with proper testimony.

Given the agricultural imagery in Polycarp's letter mentioned earlier, we might think of Polycarp's language of Christ's blood as a down payment of righteousness as parallel to the shipbuilding contracts, which also require a down payment. The Philippians, rooted in faith by Paul, have been yielding a harvest of righteousness, and this has been a long-term, multigenerational project. The Philippians are still obligated to follow right teaching and act rightly in order to continue to produce fruit. They are given the earnest money of Christ's blood to fund their labor, but that labor is still expected. Polycarp's warning about divine judgment makes sense in this broader theological economy, because the Philippians, as part of a long-term investment, are still expected to complete their contract fully and on time. The down payment offered by Christ still requires their future participation, and they will be required to render their accounts before God. For those who do not offer proper testimony, God holds them responsible for the loss of the down payment, namely, Christ's blood.[48] If the Philippians cannot follow the right example they have learned from Paul, they will be held responsible in a cosmic court for both their own sin and Christ's suffering.

There is significant risk in the Philippians' cosmic court appearance. According to Polycarp, the trial's outcome depends on the sources to which the Philippians turn for imitation and teaching. While they already have all of the resources at their disposal, including the teachings of Paul and the warranty his example provided, they could still come up short when called for judgment. This is one of the reasons why they should cede earthly arbitration to the leadership roles that Polycarp highlights, especially the presbyters, and why the categories laid out by Polycarp should follow the instructions he gives to them. Polycarp is concerned that those who are empty-minded are being led astray, and there are those who would prepare them incorrectly for their trial. Court is not a matter to be taken lightly:

Πᾶς γάρ ὃς ἂν μὴ ὁμολογῇ, Ἰησοῦν Χριστὸν ἐν σαρκὶ ἐληλυθέναι, ἀντίχριστός ἐστιν· καὶ ὃς ἂν μὴ ὁμολογῇ τὸ μαρτύριον τοῦ σταυροῦ, ἐκ τοῦ διαβόλου ἐστίν· καὶ ὃς ἂν μεθοδεύῃ τὰ λόγια τοῦ κυρίου πρὸς τὰς ἰδίας ἐπιθυμίας καὶ λέγῃ μήτε ἀνάστασιν μήτε κρίσιν, οὗτος πρωτότοκός ἐστι τοῦ σατανᾶ.

For anyone who does not confess that Jesus Christ has come in the flesh is an antichrist; and whoever does not confess the witness of the cross is from the devil; and whoever distorts the words of the Lord for his own passions, saying that there is neither resurrection nor judgment—this one is the firstborn of Satan.[49]

It is a circular argument—Polycarp uses a juridical setting to argue for the proper belief in judgment. Everyone will be called to give witness to their proper understandings about Christ, the cross, the words of the Lord, and the existence of resurrection and future judgment. Here, it becomes clear that Polycarp has turned a theo-economic framework toward an antiheresy claim. For Polycarp, rendering a proper account before God requires being in proper agreement (*homologeō*) with his understanding of correct Christian teaching.

Conclusion: The Down Payment of Righteousness

The economy of suffering in Paul's Letter to the Philippians has been expanded by a Christian writing to the descendants of those to whom Paul wrote in Philippi. Polycarp, like Paul, relies on a model in which Christ's suffering body is a commodity that can be used in a divine-human transaction in which salvation is at stake, and he deploys language about the value of that commodity in such a way that its value requires the further investment of the Philippian communities. Polycarp uses the value of the suffering body of Christ as an exemplum, and he includes other suffering bodies, including

Paul's and Ignatius's, in the valuation. Polycarp's use of Christ as a deposit for humanity's future judgment makes sense within the theo-economic logic of Paul's Letter to the Philippians, but only when read alongside the theo-economics of the Roman juridical system, in which divine judgment was possible, financial investment was required to access justice, and false testimony could incur stiff financial penalties. Polycarp deploys the down payment of Christ's suffering body to marshal authority for particular ecclesial roles (such as presbyters and martyrs), to regulate beliefs in a polemical mode, and to forward his interpretation of Paul's teaching as correct for encouraging testimony that will earn divine reward and avoid divine punishment.

Conclusion

Theo-Economies in Early Christianity

HOW DO WE READ New Testament and early Christian texts differently when we take seriously the intersections between theology and economics in Mediterranean antiquity? In this book, I have introduced just such a reading strategy, with a focus on Paul's Letter to the Philippians and one of its multiple exegetical afterlives. This strategy helps us to overcome scholarly difficulties in a variety of contemporary academic fields, including classics, archaeology, economic history, and biblical studies. Traditional separations among these fields have created silos that make invisible the intersections between theology and economics in antiquity.

On the one hand, classicists, economic historians, and archaeologists have not viewed their material evidence, including documentary and epigraphic evidence that helps us to map the ancient economy, within a religious studies framework. The result has been that scholars have not taken seriously evidence that the gods were understood as actants in the economy. Transacting with a god or goddess might bring about health, security, safe childbirth, good fortune, freedom, political advantage, social status, or even a promise of resurrection. Persons in antiquity responded to their divinities diversely and complexly, including when participating in the economy. The academic field of economics has largely moved away from a *homo economicus* model, which treats human beings as rational-choice actors, always working for their own best economic interest. However, scholars of antiquity still frequently try to consider the financial benefits accrued to those persons transacting with gods, whether selling land, signing a contract, or using a temple's banking system, even when the evidence is simply not there or the transaction results in financial loss. Instead, with a theo-economic framework, we find that a person might approach financial interactions with divine beings, their human intermediaries, and the economic structures that support them with a variety of emotions, including piety, gratitude, fear, hope, and obligation. There are more things to gain and lose than wealth when accounting for interactions with the gods in antiquity. A theo-economic framework brought to this evidence opens up new possibilities not only for understanding religion in antiquity but also for mapping the ancient economy.

On the other hand, biblical studies has not fully accounted for the divine in its consideration of economic themes. While there has been increasing interest in economic categories, including status, and a growing interest in poverty and income inequality in antiquity (particularly in Pauline studies), this scholarship has largely taken its cues from economic historians, regularly considering and reconsidering, for example, wealth-distribution models in antiquity; scholarship has focused more on quantitative than qualitative analysis. In particular, we have not adequately considered the vibrant economic lives of poor persons who would have made up the majority of the early assemblies to whom Paul wrote. A myopic focus on the poor as objects of charitable concern, and thus of scholarly study, does not engage fully with the texts and practices emerging from these assemblies. The poor in Philippi, even in their poverty, understood their relationship with one another, with other Christ assemblies, with Paul, and with God in terms of abundance. The poor should not solely be defined by their poverty, and their theology, including how they articulate their economic relationship with God, should not only be read with regard to their socioeconomic status.

The ways in which participants in the assemblies in Christ understood, used, and remixed language from the broader Greco-

Roman context deserves as much attention as the poverty of those to whom Paul wrote. Poverty in the Pauline correspondence is better understood if it is read alongside bountiful language of gain, loss, profits, abundance, security, prosperity, and venture that is found throughout the Letter to the Philippians and the other letters ascribed to Paul. The financial themes in Philippians are resonant for Paul and the Philippian communities, even if in different, not always synchronous directions. Intertwined in the financial themes of the letter are both Paul's attempt to broker between the Philippians and God and the Philippians' communal sharing. The Philippians, a collective that should not solely be defined by its poverty, provided financial, spiritual, and physical support to an imprisoned Paul even when they lacked resources. Of equal importance, they understood themselves as fully participating with God and with Paul in the divine-human partnership of the gospel, and they did not see their poverty as inhibiting their ability to contribute to the divine-human collective.[1]

Biblical studies has missed the ways in which Paul and other early Christ followers work within but also rework a system in which God transacts with humans, even the poor. My focus on theo-economics has brought evidence from the broader socioeconomic context of the ancient Mediterranean into conversation with New Testament and early Christian texts, while using a framework that allows me to ask new questions both of this socioeconomic evidence and of the texts that we study. This in turn allows biblical studies scholars to bring such new questions to the broader study of antiquity.

These broader scholarly trends represent precisely the sort of impasses that Bruno Latour said require the creation of new terms to help translate among different disciplines. I have proposed a model of theo-economics, which opens up new possibilities for exploring the entanglements between theology and the economy in the ancient world. I have coined this term precisely because our contemporary scholarly categories too often separate complex systems and realities that were not separated in antiquity. Theo-economics provides scholarly flexibility to consider a broader of range of ancient evidence that describes the ways in which humans and divinities interacted. Persons in antiquity had complex lives both economically and theologically. Given the material and literary evidence

throughout the ancient Mediterranean, it is clear that persons encountered divinities within their day-to-day financial transactions,
and they regularly deployed financial language to describe their relationships with those divinities. By examining evidence, including
material objects, beyond elite literary sources, I have been able to
explore these entanglements more expansively because of the work
of materialists such as Jane Bennett. Coins imprinted with divine
beings, imperial letters preserved in stone, and land leases scribbled
on papyrus all have very real effects on both the economic realities
and theological imaginaries of persons in antiquity.

In chapter 1, I began by focusing on these types of material objects to map out the landscape of theo-economics in antiquity. Considering a range of evidence spread over broad chronological and
geographic range demonstrates the myriad ways in which humans
and divines transacted with one another. By focusing on the type
of objects typically studied by classicists and archaeologists, including inscriptions, papyri, statues, coins, and monumental structures,
I considered a set of evidence often overlooked or treated in passing by biblical studies. I offered some initial classification for this
evidence, not to circumscribe every instantiation of divine-human
financial transactions in antiquity but to clarify two foundations for
the project. First, such evidence demonstrates—across geographical, cultural, and religious boundaries—that the phenomenon of
divine activity in the economy is ubiquitous in antiquity and would
have been legible to persons living in the first century CE. Second,
this evidence paints a picture, with broad brushstrokes, of what the
divine economy looks like in antiquity, affording us a view into how
theo-economics helps us to understand both theological and economic logics that would have been legible to the earliest Christ followers. By mapping out this evidence, scholars begin to have a way
to imagine the resonances invoked by financial language deployed
in relationship to God or Christ in New Testament and early Christian texts.

I discussed aspects of this theo-economic taxonomy by considering two types of evidence. First, I considered the role of temples
and other cultic sites as financial institutions, including as banking
centers, storage sites, and property managers. Within temple institutions, the gods are often understood as owning property and man-

aging wealth, and cultic officials play an important role in mediating these transactions and overseeing the investment and distribution of divine wealth. Cultic sites are also economic sites, and both gods and humans do business in temples, from the transactions of sacrifice to sacred storage to manumission contracts. Evidence from Greco-Roman temples and synagogues throughout the Mediterranean shows that both Jews and practitioners of various Greco-Roman religions understood the divine as an active financial actor within sacred spaces.

The gods are also present in what we might consider solely business settings. I also examined evidence for the presence of the gods in noncultic spaces, focusing on inscriptions and statues found in commercial spaces, including *makella*, or marketplaces. Gods, especially Hermes, are frequently invoked in image and text as overseeing and regulating the transactions occurring within commercial spaces. Divine and divinized beings are also represented on currency and weight standards. The gods not only are participants in temple business, or even just invoked in the statuary and inscriptions of commercial spaces, but are also present on the very media of exchange. Divine and semidivine figures are found regulating the financial pipework of the ancient economy and on the currency itself. These objects are also often vehicles for imperial ideology, as is clear from the colonization coinage from Philippi. It is clear that brokering the divine has significant power, status, and wealth at stake. But most persons, whether elite or nonelite, when paying taxes, making a down payment on a camel, receiving wages, or even simply purchasing groceries, would use legal tender that invoked both imperial and divine power.

With this theo-economic context as foundation, chapter 2 turned to the first-century CE letter from Paul to the Christ followers at Philippi. This letter, unlike other Pauline correspondence, uses the term *koinōnia* (venture) and not *ekklēsia* (assembly) as the primary term to describe the community of Christ followers at Philippi, Paul and Timothy's relationship to them, and their mutual relationship with God and Christ in the gospel. The primary framework for understanding this letter and the community to which it is written is not only political but also theo-economic. Using recent work by Julien Ogereau, I provided evidence that *koinōnia*, which has frequently been translated in a watered-down way as "fellowship," is regularly used for contracts, including land leases and marriage agreements, and carries connotations of a situation in which there is shared risk of loss and reward. In a letter in which the support (including financial support) of Paul in prison is a major theme, the use of the multivalent language of *koinōnia* should be read with its financial connotations at the fore. By examining some of these everyday legal and financial comparanda, I considered the rhetorical implications of a "*koinōnia* in the gospel" (Phil 1:5). Paul writes that he has a venture in the gospel with the Philippians, who are described as a divine worksite where work will be completed on time by the day of Christ (Phil 1:5–6), and the Philippians are a divine field that will yield a harvest of righteousness (Phil 1:11).

Reading Philippians 1 with a focus on *koinōnia* helps to explain other language in the chapter that has largely puzzled commentators, for example, the claim that "living is Christ and dying is gain" (Phil 1:21). If the gospel is a venture in which the Philippians and Paul share in risk and reward, then Paul's description of his imprisonment as happening for the *prokopē*, or progress, of the gospel (Phil 1:12) should be read within the theo-economic context of the gospel venture in which Paul and the Philippians participate. Paul first mentions his imprisonment in 1:7 by claiming it is in the defense (*apologia*) and security (*bebaiōsis*) of the gospel. A focus on the latter term, *bebaiōsis*, security, took up the second half of the chapter. Unlike commentators who, following Adolf Deissmann, have tried to pair *bebaiōsis* with *apologia* as a formal legal term, I argued that it makes more sense to take *bebaiōsis* in the context of its nearly ubiquitous use in contracts to indicate warranties or securities in business transactions. Securities can be both physical property and persons (often slaves are lumped together with other properties in securing loans). Thus, Paul is offering his imprisoned body as his contribution to the progress of the gospel venture. In circumstances in which the Philippians are providing support, including probably financial support, for Paul during his imprisonment, Paul could have been perceived as causing loss to the gospel venture. To offset that perception, Paul, who identifies as a slave of Christ at the letter's opening, claims to be the security for the gospel venture. I concluded that, in doing so, Paul continues to assert himself as a mediator between God and the Philippians in the gospel venture, because only he can guarantee the gospel's success through his imprisonment.

I concluded by turning to Philippians 4, in which Paul gives grudging thanks for the financial support from the Philippian communities that have partnered with him in the past in "the matter of giving and receiving." A focus on human-human financial relationships has hampered a full reading of Phil 4:19, where Paul offers a divine promissory note to the Philippians. The result is a broadly conceived divine-human economy in which, while Paul and the Philippians are in a joint venture, Paul continues to reassert his position as their divine-human theo-economic intermediary by claiming that he is the one who can call in divine favor to make up for any support they have offered him through Epaphroditus. By considering these two chapters, which are tied by linguistic similarities, it becomes clear that financial support, labor, and human suffering are intertwined in the letter. This reveals an early Christ-following theo-economy in which abundance can be found in lack and loss, giving produces receiving, and, despite these quasi-utopian upendings of traditional economic systems, Paul continues to try to insinuate himself as God's broker to the Philippians.

Chapter 3 turned to the cluster of financial terms in Phil 3:7–11, asking in particular how we should read Phil 3:8, which describes a divine tally sheet in which Paul counts all of his gains as loss "so that he might gain the profit Christ." By considering this language within the framework of theo-economics, I was able to expand my analysis not only to consider the gods as economic actors who control traditionally economic resources such as land and money but also to consider the broader theo-economic system in which theological resources are also commodified and in which theological resources are controlled by divine beings and their human intermediaries. To do this, I compared the accounting language of Phil 3:7–11, in which Paul describes a theological accounting system in which Christ is a profitable resource, to literary and epigraphic comparanda, including Lucian's *Lives for Sale*, a work in which humans and gods participate in the purchase of human and divine figures. Access to the gods and the gods themselves function as a commodity that can be bought, sold, and traded. I connected Phil 3:7–11, where Christ is commodified, with Phil 2, which depicts Christ as having the form of a slave. Through this reading of Philippians 2–3, I showed that an analysis of economics in antiquity should not only consider typical questions of access to and control of resources such as land, food, water, and money but also begin to consider theological questions about access to and control of theological resources such as healing, righteousness, and resurrection from the dead. Thus, a theo-economic framework contributes both to biblical studies and to broader conversations in religious studies, classics, and economic history. Toward the end of the chapter, I considered how Phil 3:7–11 connects with other commodified theological resources within the letter, especially the valuation of suffering. Cases such as Paul's *koinōnia* in suffering with Christ, his discussion of the profitability of dying in Philippians 1, and the way in which Epaphroditus's labor, illness, and near death fill a perceived debt in Philippians 2 show how human bodies and the suffering and illness they endure are tallied up when considering theological access to Christ, resurrection, and God.

Chapter 4 followed one thread in the multiple afterlives of the theo-economic language in the Letter to the Philippians. I considered how a later text, Polycarp's *Letter to the Philippians*, depicts Christ and suffering. When we pay attention to Polycarp's use of some of the same theo-economic themes deployed by Paul in his letter to this same community, it becomes clear that there is an important theo-economic logic that ties together the letter's focus on the use and misuse of money, exegesis of texts such as 1 Tim 6:10, concerns over false teaching, and emphasis on God's judgment. I considered these themes alongside a reading of Pol. *Phil.* 8.1–2, where Polycarp introduces the idea that Christ is the "down payment for our righteousness."

Polycarp uses a juridical setting of divine judgment to claim that everyone will be called to render accounts before God, which will be adjudicated against the down payment of Christ's blood. Failure to have proper understandings about Christ, the cross, the words of the Lord, and the existence of resurrection and future judgment incur responsibility not only for the individual but for the loss of the initial *arrabōn*, down payment, of Christ. This juridical language can best be understood in light of contracts involving down payments, including a first-century CE petition for imperial response from Kos, where the sacred judgment of the emperor requires going through intermediary channels and furnishing an *arrabōn* to demonstrate adequate financing to follow through with the petitioners' appeal. Juridical contexts are the site of theo-economic thinking in early Christianity, too, especially within the context of the empire. The theo-economic logic of the language of down payment is therefore legible in a text whose primary concern seems to be related to cosmic judgment. I concluded that Polycarp interprets the theo-economic logic of Philippians 3 and argues that the suffering Christ-body on the cross is now a commodity that has the value level of a down payment for humanity's sins. If the Philippians cannot follow the right example they have learned from Paul, they will be held responsible in a cosmic court for the full amount due, which includes both their own sin and Christ's suffering. The commodification of Christ has been turned to polemical ends. This text demonstrates the economic logics at work in developing christologies and theologies of suffering.

My intention with this project has been to lay the foundation for a new methodology with implications for New Testament studies, the study of early Christianity, and the study of religion more broadly. By working with the framework of divine activity in the economy, we are able to read New Testament and early Christian texts with a new lens that highlights the transactional entanglements of human and divine beings. This reading strategy does not need to be limited to the Letter to the Philippians, or even to the letters of Paul, but can also be used for other texts. A theo-economic methodology helps us to ask new questions of the texts we study, so that arguments about care for the poor, poverty, income inequality, and social status are asked alongside questions that imagine new possibilities for the way these texts figure human-human and human-divine transactions. Topics that have traditionally been understood as solely theological (cosmology, creation, incarnation, self-knowledge, divine judgment) should be examined as part of a broader divine economy that is not separate from topics that relate to matters of day-to-day lives, including the financial lives, of early Christ followers.

Theo-economics can be useful for a variety of early Christian literature. Within the letters of Paul, to take one example, *koinōnia* occurs in Romans, 1 and 2 Corinthians, Galatians, and Philemon.[2] From parables in the gospels in which God is described as a demanding estate owner who obligates followers to provide a return on divine investment or to face judgment (cf. Matt 25:14–30; Luke 19:12–27) to the sayings in the Gospel of Thomas, in which ack of self-knowledge is described as a poverty and incarnation is described as wealth dwelling in poverty, there is also significant potential outside the letters of Paul. Many New Testament and early Christian texts intertwine what has traditionally been understood solely as a theological topic with the financial language we find in the broader theo-economy of the Roman Empire, that is, in legal or financial documents that sometimes involve divine beings. Our understanding of each of these texts—and no doubt of others, as well—could benefit from considering the theo-economics they contain.

Expanding to a broader range of early Christian literature will provide additional data for understanding the theological and economic entanglements of early Christianity. Just as there is no monolithic "early Christian" way to understand marriage or the resurrection body or leadership structures, so too there are multiple ways in which early Christ followers and the generations that came after them understood their own financial practices, their transactions with God, and their use of financial language in their theological imaginaries. Chapters 3 and 4 demonstrated the sort of diachronic work that can be done, tracing one interpretation of Paul's commodification of suffering. A much broader study could productively analyze the deployment of theo-economic language, especially as it relates to suffering, across a wider set of early Christian literature. I am interested in the ways that both human suffering and flourishing are assigned value in a system where divine-human brokers attempt to set the theological and practical standards for access to God. My project has shown that there is evidence for an economy of suffering developing in early Christianity. A theo-economic framework can illuminate how this economy of suffering functions and help to explain the use and value of texts that commodify human and divine suffering.

Given the diverse ways in which contemporary Christians are responding, for example, to the human suffering and economic devastation wreaked by the current COVID-19 pandemic, it seems ethically urgent to understand better the ways in which early Christians understood the economy as deeply entangled with theology in order to make sense of human suffering and flourishing. As some Christians collect and distribute resources for persons left devastated by this pandemic while holding virtual worship services, others defy stay-at-home orders and encourage followers to continue to gather in large groups, and both groups deploy theologies about human suffering to do so.[3] Still others are pushing for rapid return to normalcy, writing pieces about human sacrifice for the good of the economy.[4] How would an exploration of the diversity of early Christian economies of suffering help to understand, explain, and perhaps even critique these responses in our current moment?

Acts of the Apostles is another especially fruitful text for theo-economics as a methodological strategy. While there has been significant scholarship on the themes of wealth and poverty in Luke-Acts, there is a broader range of questions that arise from a theo-economic framework, when God is taken seriously as an economic actor in Acts.[5] The story of Ananias and Sapphira in Acts 5:1–11, for example, raises the question, What are the theological and economic consequences of depicting God as the violent price-check on a property sale? This story depicts God as the financial enforcer, invoked by Peter, of the practices of the *ekklēsia*. What would it mean to read this narrative alongside other property sales and disputes that invoke the divine?[6] A focus on divine-human transactions, brokered through the figure of Peter, complicates the scholarly depictions of the economic themes of Acts and this story as a contrast to Acts 2. A theo-economic framework for Acts 5 also raises a broader question about the ways in which gender, too, is entangled with economics and theology in Acts.[7] The portrayals of Lydia and the enslaved girl telling fortunes in Acts 16 reveal the ways in which women are often rhetorically framed in terms of their productivity, which in Acts 16 is used as a foil to highlight Paul's power and persuasion and God's divine intervention on his behalf. Given that women regularly exercise religious leadership in Greco-Roman religions, what does it mean that Acts regularly portrays women in relation to their contributions to the *ekklēsia* and the work of male apostles such as Peter and Paul?

This subject raises the need for further work on the way early Christianity depicts the intersections of gender, theology, and economics. Moreover, given that the household is the base economic unit in antiquity, we find a variety of anxieties around women's production and reproduction, labor, wealth and property ownership, and control over their own financial decisions, including patronage, charity, and personal spending. It is clear that the ancient theo-economy is frequently gendered, and we find numerous examples where women's financial behavior is used as a rhetorical device to reflect on the masculinity of their spouses. How do New Testament and early Christian texts (particularly, for example, the Pastoral Epistles) participate in and respond to these broader gendered theo-economic concerns? To take a single example, Cyprian's *On the Dress of Virgins* uses language of lending on interest (*faeneror*) to God to describe how Cyprian would like women to use their property to invest in the church (through charity), intertwining attempts to assert episcopal authority over women's dress, property, and practices by using lending language to set up Cyprian as a divine-human intermediary. Women transact with and broker for the gods in the broader divine-human economy, and individuals and systems attempt to circumscribe women's role in the various divine-human economies of antiquity. A theo-economic framework might help to open up new directions in the analysis of women's religious leadership in antiquity and help to explain the frequent overlap between concerns over women's wealth and arguments about ecclesial structures. As comparing Paul's Letter to the Philippians and Polycarp's *Letter to the Philippians* helped to trace one of many afterlives of the theo-economic themes present in early Christianity, a broader study compiling evidence from several texts and contexts would begin to untangle the diverse ways in which gender, economy, and theology are intertwined in early Christianity.

Archives of Divine-Human Economies

This book is also participating in emerging interdisciplinary conversations that have turned to evidence from early Christianity to consider everything from contemporary U.S. religious practices to political theology to philosophy. Scholars in a variety of disciplines have begun to take more seriously the overlaps between theology and economics by turning to sources from antiquity. To take a few examples, Jacques Rancière's *The Philosopher and His Poor* provides "a history of formal thinking about the poor"[8] and considers the ways in which thinkers both ancient and modern have figured the poor as objects of analysis or illustrations for philosophical argument. Giorgio Agamben, like Foucault and the genealogical tradition, explores contemporary society by tracing earlier philosophical and political moments. In *The Kingdom and the Glory*, Agamben explores the ways in which certain strains of Christian theology, namely, the imagery of God (as Father) managing a divine household, or *oikonomia*, come to undergird the modern economic state. These intersections between theology and economics have drawn significant attention to texts and traditions from late antiquity, including the work of Peter Brown, Helen Rhee, and Devin Singh, among others.[9] What I hope my project shows is that there is additional evidence available from the earliest literature of Christianity; that there are multiple, complex ways in which early Christ followers understood God's activity in their financial practices; and that there are possibilities beyond human wealth and poverty among the theological and economic imaginaries of early Christianity.

The intersections of theology and economics have drawn increasing interest as well from religious studies more broadly. From the relationship between mass media and the prosperity gospel to the interwoven threads of TV bingeing, meditation, and fundamentalism, scholars whose work considers contemporary religion have explored the ways in which an interest in economic themes opens up new possibilities for understanding the practice of religion.[10] I hope that my project demonstrates that the divisions between theology and economy reflect contemporary scholarly disciplines more than ancient realities. I hope that this contributes to a larger conversation in the study of religion about inter- and transdisciplinary possibilities that ultimately better represent the persons, communities, institutions, texts, and objects that we study. Kathryn Lofton offers one model for the potential of this type of work. "*Consuming Religion* thinks about the marketplace as the primary archive of religion."[11] If the marketplace can be the primary archive of religion in antiquity, and I think it can, it must be imagined as an open-air space, capable of accounting for both the lofty divine heights and the mundane business of camel sales and land leases.

This book began with the image of a checkbook featuring a quotation from Phil 4:13, which helped me consider the ways in which entangled theological and economic logics are at work in this object. With this checkbook in mind, when I imagine the open-air archive of religion in antiquity, I think of the broken limestone measuring table from Kipia, some fifteen kilometers southwest of Philippi, which we first considered in chapter 1.[12] This pierced table top with two circular cavities was used to follow a standard when measuring goods. The table contains three brief lines of Latin:

[. . . I]I . uir . s(ua) . p(ecunia) . f(aciendum) c (urauit).
Pro [sa]lute . col(oniae) . Iul(iae) . Aug(ustae) . Philippi-
    ens(ium) .
Heroi . A[ulo]nite . sacr(um).

(an unknown) duumvir erected (this table) at his own
    expense.
For the well-being of the colony Julia Augusta of the
    Philippiens.
Consecrated to the Thracian Horseman.[13]

A *duumvir*, a Roman official, dedicates a limestone table for the well-being of the colony at Philippi. This table is both functional and theological. It is, on the one hand, used to measure merchandise to ensure that transactions are fair and equitable. But this table is also theological; it and its work are consecrated to an important local deity. This measuring table and its dedicatory inscription are similar to the two previously discussed statue bases offered by aediles to imperial equity found in the *makellon* at Philippi.[14] The bronze statues, rendered from the melted-down metal of confiscated improper measuring weights, would have represented Hermes and imperial equity.

I think the archive of religion in antiquity must be expansive enough to include objects like this table and these statue bases as well as texts such as the Letter to the Philippians. People moved through spaces alive with divine beings and imperial bureaucracy in day-to-day financial transactions, including even the purchase of a small measure of grain, poured through this table. Whether or not grain ended up offered at an altar or consumed in a dining room, both theological and economic practices affected the grain's journey. From the divinized emperor's visage stamped on the coin that was exchanged for it to the authority of the deity invoked to measure it to the bronze figure of a god looming nearby, a person encountered the vibrant materiality of the divine in these transactions; the archive of religion in antiquity is a theo-economic system. Divine beings, too, were vibrantly alive in letters circulated and read and heard among the communities dedicated to them, in the collective resources shared, in the support offered in the midst of suffering, and in both abundance and lack. The archive of religion in antiquity must be able to describe this full range of the intersections of theology and economy. For scholars in disciplines still too often siloed from one another, cataloging such an archive requires new language that can provide an accounting of not only human economic activity but also divine.

Appendix:
A Theo-Economic Translation
of the Letter to the Philippians

AS I WAS PREPARING the book, it became clear that it was necessary to create a fresh translation of the Letter to the Philippians that highlights language that has financial valences. While not every word that has a financial connotation *must* be read that way, reading with a heavy leaning in this direction offers a new perspective that highlights aspects of the letter that are often overlooked. For the text of the New Testament, I rely on Nestle et al., *Novum Testamentum Graece*.

Philippians 1

Paul and Timothy, slaves of Christ Jesus to all the holy ones in Christ Jesus who are in Philippi, together with the overseers and the helpers, grace to you and peace from God our Father and the Lord Jesus Christ. I give thanks to my God in every remembrance of you, always in every one of my supplications on behalf of all of you, making supplication with joy because of your venture in the gospel from the first day until now. I have confidence in this, that the one who began a good work in you will complete it by the day of Jesus Christ. Even as it is right for me to think this way about all of you because I have you in my heart, both in my imprisonment and in my defense and warranty of the gospel, since all of you are my joint shareholders in grace. For God is my witness how I long for you with the affections of Christ Jesus. And I pray this, that your love will have more and more left over in knowledge and in every insight to help you determine the best things, so that you may be pure and blameless on the day of Christ, having yielded the harvest of righteousness that is through Jesus Christ for the glory and approval of God.[1]

I want you to know, brothers and sisters, that the things that have happened to me have happened for the progress of the gospel, so that my imprisonment in Christ has become clearly known to the whole *praitōrion* and to all the rest, and most of my brothers and sisters in the Lord have been made confident by my imprisonment to speak the word more abundantly and without fear. Some proclaim Christ through envy and rivalry, but some others proclaim Christ through goodwill. Some [proclaim Christ] out of love, knowing that I am deposited for the defense of the gospel, but others declare Christ out of self-interest, impurely, intending to stir up suffering by my imprisonment. What does it matter? Only that in every way, whether by pretext or true motive, Christ is declared, and in that I rejoice. Yes, and I will continue to rejoice, for I know that this will turn out for my security through your supplications and through the supply of the spirit of Jesus Christ in accordance with my eager expectation and my hope, that in no way will I be tarnished, but in all boldness of speech as always and even now Christ will be magnified in my body, whether through life or through death. For me, living is Christ and dying is gain. For if I am living in the flesh, this is a fruitful work for me, and what I prefer I do not know. I am constrained between the two, having a desire to depart and to be with Christ, for that is much better. But to remain in the flesh is more necessary for you. Since I am confident in this, I know that I will remain and endure with all of you for your progress and joy of faith, so that your boasting may abound in Christ Jesus in me through my coming again to you.

Only, make your dealings worthy of the gospel of Jesus Christ, so that whether coming and seeing you or being absent I hear about the things concerning you, that you are standing firm in one spirit, striving together in one soul in the faith of the gospel and not being frightened in any way by those who are set against you. For them this is an indication of destruction, but of your security, and this is from God, that it has been granted to you as a favor concerning Christ, not only to have trust in him but also to suffer for him, having the same struggle that you saw in me and that you hear is still in me.

Philippians 2

If there is any appeal in Christ, any encouragement from love, any spirit-venture, any affection and compassion, render my joy in full, so that you have the same mind, having the same love, being united, keeping one thing in mind; do nothing from self-interest[2] or conceit but in humility, considering others above yourself. Let each of you not look to your own things but also to the things of others. Have this mind in you that was also in Christ Jesus, who, despite existing in the form of God, did not consider being equal with God ἁρπαγμὸν[3] but emptied himself, taking the form of a slave being born in the likeness of humans, and being found in form like a human, he lessened himself, becoming obedient to the point of death, even death on a cross. Therefore God also highly exalted him and granted to him the name that is over every name, so that at the name of Jesus every knee should bend from the heavens and from the earth and from under the earth, and every tongue should confess that Jesus Christ is lord to the glory of God the Father.

Therefore, my beloved, just as you always have obeyed, not only in my presence but also now much more in my absence, with fear and trembling achieve with labor your own salvation. For it is God who is working in you both to will and to work for his goodwill. Do everything without murmuring and without balancing your accounts, so that you might be blameless and pure, unblemished children of God in the middle of a crooked and twisted generation, in which you shine like stars in the world. By your offering the word of life, I can boast on the day of Christ that I have not run empty-handed, nor have I labored empty-handed. But even if I am poured out as a drink offering for the sacrifice and service of your credit, I rejoice and I rejoice together with you. In the same way also rejoice and rejoice together with me.

I hope in the Lord Jesus to send Timothy to you soon, so that I might also be encouraged by the things concerning you. For I have no one else like-minded who will genuinely take care for the things concerning you. For all of them are seeking things for themselves, not the things of Christ Jesus. But you know his worth, that, as a child with its father, he has slaved together with me in the gospel. I hope then to send him as soon as I have seen how things turn out for me, and I am persuaded in the Lord that I will come myself soon.

Still, I considered it necessary to send to you Epaphroditus, my brother and coworker and fellow soldier, a messenger and servant of my needs, since he was longing to see all of you, and he was anguished because you heard that he was ill. He was really sick and almost died, but God had mercy on him, not only on him but also on me, so that I would not have sorrow upon sorrow. Therefore I am even more eager to send him, so that having seen him again, you would rejoice, and I might be less anxious. Receive him, then, in the Lord, with all joy, and honor such people, because he came near to death for the work of Christ, disregarding his life, so that he might fill up your deficit of service to me.

Philippians 3

Finally, my sisters and brothers, rejoice in the Lord. To write the same things to you is not troublesome for me, and to you it is an assurance. Beware the dogs, beware the evil workers. Beware the mutilation. For we are the circumcision who worship the spirit of God and glorify Christ Jesus, not trusting in the flesh. Although I also have confidence in the flesh. If anyone else thinks to have confidence in the flesh, I have more. Circumcised on the eighth day, a member of the people of Israel, of the tribe of Benjamin, a Hebrew of Hebrews; as to the law, a Pharisee; as to zeal, a persecutor of the church; as to righteousness under the law, blameless.

But whatever was for me a gain, these things I calculated as a loss on account of Christ. But even more I calculate that all things are a loss on account of the better value of the knowledge of Christ Jesus my Lord, on whose account I counted all things as a loss, and I considered them dung, so that I might gain the profit Christ and be wealthy in him, not having my righteousness that is from the law but that is through faith in Christ, which is a righteousness from God in faith, in order to know him and the power of his resurrection and a venture in his sufferings, being conformed to his death, if somehow I might attain resurrection from the dead.

Not that I already have obtained it or that I have already been perfected, but I pursue it to make it my own, if I might seize it, just as I have been seized by Christ Jesus. Brothers and sisters, I do not think that I have taken it myself, but forgetting the things that lie behind and reaching for the things that lie ahead, I pursue the aim of the prize of the heavenly calling in Christ Jesus. Let the ones who are mature have the same mind, and if any of you think differently, God will still reveal this to you. Only hold fast to that which we have attained.

Become imitators of me, brothers and sisters, and consider those who are living in this way, just as you have a pattern from us. For many are living about whom I told you, and now even while weeping, that I say are enemies of the cross of Christ, whose end is destruction, whose God is the belly, and whose glory is in their shame. They have in mind earthly things, but our citizenship exists in heaven, from where we await a savior, the Lord Jesus Christ. He will transform our lowered body, so that it may be conformed to his glory body, according to his ability to work to make all things subject to him.

Philippians 4

Therefore, my brothers and sisters, whom I love and long for, my joy and my crown, stand in the Lord, beloved. I greet Euodia and Syntychē, to be like-minded in the Lord. Yes, I say to you, my genuine colleagues, help these women, for they labor together in the gospel with me and also with Clement and with the rest of my co-workers, whose names are in the book of life.

Always rejoice in the Lord. I say again, rejoice. Let your fairness be known to all people. The Lord is near. Do not worry at all, but in every petition and supplication with thanksgiving let your requests be known to the Lord. And the peace of God that exceeds all knowing will keep watch over your hearts and your minds in Christ Jesus.

Finally, whatever is true, whatever is holy, whatever is pure, whatever is pleasing, whatever is well-spoken, if there is any excellence, if there is anything commendable, consider these things. The things that you have learned and received and heard and known in me, do these things. And the God of peace will be with you.

I rejoice greatly in the Lord that at last you revived your concern for me, about which you also were concerned, even though you were without opportunity. Not that I speak about lack, for I have learned to be self-sufficient in these things. For I know how to have little, and I know how to abound. But in any and all things I have learned both to be full and to hunger, both to be abundant and to be lacking. I am strong in all things in the one who strengthened me.

Yet you did well by having a joint share with me in suffering. And you know, Philippians, that in the beginning of the gospel, when I came from Macedonia, that no assembly ventured with me in the matter of giving and receiving except you alone. Even in Thessaloniki you sent not only once but twice for my need. Not that I sought the gift, but I sought the fruit that accumulated to your account. I have received everything in full, and I have more than enough. I have been fulfilled, having received from Epaphroditus the things from you, a fragrant offering, an acceptable sacrifice, pleasing to God. And my God will fulfill all your lack according to his riches in glory in Christ Jesus. Glory be to God our Father forever and ever, amen.

Greet every holy one in Christ Jesus. The brothers and sisters who are with me greet you. The holy ones greet you, especially those from the household of Caesar. The gift of the Lord Jesus Christ be with your spirit.

Abbreviations

IN THIS BOOK, I use the standard abbreviations for journal titles, book series, and primary sources laid out in *The SBL Handbook of Style*, 2nd ed. (Atlanta: SBL Press, 2014). All titles not listed in this handbook have been presented in full. For inscriptions, I follow Horsley and Lee, "Preliminary Checklist"; for papyri, I follow Oates et al., *Checklist of Editions*. For ease of reference, I list the relevant abbreviations here. For the text of the New Testament, I rely on Nestle et al., *Novum Testamentum Graece*.

BGU	*Aegyptische Urkunden aus den Königlichen Museen zu Berlin, Griechische Urkunden*, vol. 1 (Berlin: Weidmannsche Buchhandlung, 1895)
CIPh 2	Cédric Brélaz, ed., *Corpus des inscriptions grecques et latines de Philippi*, vol. 2, *La colonie romaine*; Part 1, *La vie publique de la colonie*, Études épigraphiques 6 (Athens: École française d'Athènes, 2014)
FD 3	Emile Bourguet, ed., *Fouilles de Delphes*, vol. 3, *Epigraphie* (Paris: Ecole française d'Athènes, 1910–32)
IG	Friedrich Hiller von Gaertringen et al., eds., *Inscriptiones Graecae*, 14 vols. (Berlin: Reimer; de Gruyter, 1873–present)
IJO	David Noy, Alexander Panayotow, and Hanswulf Bloedhorn, eds., *Inscriptiones Judaicae Orientis*, vol. 1, *Eastern Europe*, TSAJ 101 (Tübingen: Mohr Siebeck, 2004)

JJP   *Journal of Juristic Papyrology* (1946–2010)

IKafizin   Terence B. Mitford, ed., *The Nymphaeum of Kafizin:*
                The Inscribed Pottery, Kadmos Supplement 2 (Berlin:
                de Gruyter, 1980)

LSJ   Henry George Liddell, Robert Scott, and Henry
                Stuart Jones, eds., *A Greek-English Lexicon*, 9th ed.
                with revised supplement (Oxford: Oxford Univer-
                sity Press, 1996)

P.Col.   Roger S. Bagnall, T. T. Renner, and Klaas A. Worp,
                eds., *Columbia Papyri*, vol. 8, American Studies
                in Papyrology 28 (Atlanta: American Society of
                Papyrologists, 1990); Roger S. Bagnall and Dirk
                D. Obbink, eds., *Columbia Papyri*, vol. 10, American
                Studies in Papyrology 34 (Atlanta: American Soci-
                ety of Papyrologists, 1996)

P.Flor.   Girolamo Vitelli, ed., *Papiri greco-egizii: Papiri*
                Fiorentini, 3 vols. (Milan: U. Hoepli, 1906–15)

P.Mich.   E. M. Husselman, A. E. R. Boak, and W. F. Edger-
                ton, eds., *Michigan Papyri*, vol. 5, *Papyri from*
                Tebtunis, Part II, University of Michigan Studies,
                Humanistic Series 29 (Ann Arbor: University of
                Michigan Press, 1944)

P.Mich.inv.   University of Michigan Library Digital Collec-
                tions, Advanced Papyrological Information System
                (APIS UM)

P.Mich.Mchl   E. M. Michael, ed., *A Critical Edition of Select Mich-*
                igan Papyri (Ann Arbor: University of Michigan,
                1966)

P.Oslo   Samson Eitrem and Leiv Amundsen, eds., *Papyri*
                Osloenses, vol. 3 (Oslo: Jacob Dybwad, 1936)

RIC   Harold Mattingly et al., eds., *The Roman Imperial*
                Coinage, 10 vols. (London: Spink, 1923–94)

SB   *Sammelbuch griechischer Urkunden aus Aegypten*,
                vol. 24 (Wiesbaden: Harrassowitz, 2003)

SEG   Supplementum Epigraphicum Graecum 1–63
                (1923–2017)

ZPE   *Zeitschrift für Papyrologie und Epigraphik*
                (1967–2018)

Notes

Introduction

1. Delreal, "Occupy Protest Shuts Down Harvard Yard."
2. Min, "Occupy Wall Street and Deliberative Decision-Making."
3. The Simple Way, "12 Marks of New Monasticism."
4. Worthen, "Onward Christian Healthcare?"
5. Oppenheimer, "'Christian Economics' Meets the Antiunion Movement."
6. Bowler, *Blessed*.
7. Christian Art Gifts, "Leather Checkbook Cover." My gratitude to Margaret Butterfield, who found this checkbook for sale and directed my attention to it, and to Karen Mancinelli-Page, for her excellent photography.
8. David Wilhite coined this term in a chapter on Tertullian's interpretation of Paul in *Ad uxorem*. Wilhite, "Tertullian on Widows," 222–24. Wilhite calls for a resistance against "modernist dichotomies . . . between religion and economics," in order to "read Tertullian as very much concerned with both economic issues and religious ones—the line between the two often being imperceptible" (224). While I agree with Wilhite's move to resist modernist dichotomies, his analysis is largely limited to human-human transactions, in this case, Tertullian's rhetoric about ecclesial care for widows and orphans. God's role in participating financially with the church goes largely unconsidered. To take a single example, Wilhite notes the language Tertullian uses of widows as married to God, offering "prayers as dowries" and receiving compensation in the form of imperishable goods," but does not explore further the implications of considering God as not only a husband but participating in a financial exchange with widows (prayers for imperishable goods) (233). The implications of this rhetoric reach beyond Tertullian's interpretation of Paul or ecclesiology to make strong claims about divine activity in human economics, a divine economy with its own commodities and transactions, and the ability of humans to affect activity within that divine economy.

9. Latour, *We Have Never Been Modern*, 3.
10. Here I am using "religion" to indicate the academic field of religious studies rather than "religion" as a formal category for antiquity, which scholars such as Carlin Barton and Daniel Boyarin have taught us is anachronistic (*Imagine No Religion*).
11. Latour, *We Have Never Been Modern*, 145.
12. Bennett, *Vibrant Matter*, 122.
13. Bennett, 3.
14. I am using "metaphor" here in the way it is often used, after the cognitive linguistic turn in biblical scholarship: "systematic correspondences between two conceptual domains" reveal the metaphorical relationship of these two spheres in linguistic expression. Job Y. Jindo summarizes the elements of metaphor in this model: "(1) conceptuality—metaphorical linguistic utterances are manifestations of metaphorical concepts and the conceptual world of language users; (2) systematicity—elements of one conceptual domain are systematically mapped onto the elements of another domain; (3) ubiquity—metaphor is ubiquitous in everyday discourse, not limited to a specific aesthetic discourse such as poetry or oratory; (4) fundamentality—metaphor, in many cases, operates subconsciously and remains unnoticed by language users, and yet it is fundamental to the cognitive activity of human beings and ultimately to the conceptualization of reality" ("Metaphor Theory and Biblical Texts").

    While, at first glance, theo-economic language might seem ripe for a cognitive metaphorical analysis, the evidence of real-world financial transactions between divine and human beings means that this language fails in terms of conceptuality: these transactions reflect more than metaphorical concepts. When divine beings are party to legally binding contracts with humans, own property, and keep bank accounts, the transactions reflect more than concepts. It fails in terms of systematicity: theology and economics are not two conceptual words being mapped onto each other linguistically but rather are inherently intertwined in antiquity. The financial transactions, from sacrifice to manumission to banking, which occur at cultic sites and the theological interactions present in public marketplaces demonstrate this intertwining. Finally, it fails in terms of fundamentality: these transactions are not subconscious or unnoticed, but rather they are an open and integral part of local and imperial economic structures. From coins and weight standards to building programs and taxation systems, gods and humans regularly interact at all levels of bureaucracy. For more on the evidence for theo-economics, see chapter 1. I have found that work from feminist materialists offers a better framework for exploring the effects of theo-economics in the ancient world.
15. S. Friesen, "Poverty in Pauline Studies," 323.
16. Friesen, James, and Schowalter, "Inequality in Corinth"; Oakes, "Economic Situation of the Philippian Christians." There have been several

scholarly adjustments to and disagreements about the "poverty scale" Friesen suggested. See Schiedel and Friesen, "Size of the Economy"; Longenecker, "Exposing the Economic Middle." For a broader introduction, see Atkins and Osborne, *Poverty in the Roman World.*

17. An important example of this work is Thomas R. Blanton IV and Raymond Pickett, eds., *Paul and Economics.* These fourteen essays take up important and wide-ranging topics, from Jinyu Liu's exploration of the conditions of urban poverty to Ulrike Roth's engagement with the issue of the reliance of Pauline collectives on enslaved labor. With the exception of Blanton's chapter, however, these essays focus on human-human transactions and their economic implications and do not take into account the role of the divine. For more on Blanton's work, see the following section of this introduction, "Paul and Gift Exchange."

18. Briones, *Paul's Financial Policy.*

19. Ben Witherington III and Bruce Longenecker argue for a consistent Pauline approach to poverty. Witherington, *Friendship and Finances;* Longenecker, *Remember the Poor.* See also Briones, *Paul's Financial Policy.* For some of the limitations of this approach, see Welborn, review of *Remember the Poor.*

20. These ideas are also developed in Quigley and Nasrallah, "Cost and Abundance."

21. Acts 18:1–4.

22. Sampley, *Pauline Partnership in Christ,* 84. See also Peterlin, *Paul's Letter to the Philippians.*

23. This view, espoused as early as Gustav Adolf Deissmann in 1912 (*St. Paul*), is also upheld by several scholars today, including Ascough, *Paul's Macedonian Associations,* 153.

24. E.g., Witherington, *Friendship and Finances,* 123–24; Briones, *Paul's Financial Policy,* 22–24.

25. Dodd, *New Testament Studies,* 71.

26. Dodd, 71–72.

27. Hengel with Deines, *Pre-Christian Paul.*

28. E.g., Hock, *Social Context of Paul's Ministry.*

29. Still, "Did Paul Loathe Manual Labor?," 782, Ogereau, *Paul's Koinōnia,* 3.

30. For more on the theo-economic context of *koinōnia,* see chapter 2.

31. Julien M. Ogereau has explored some of the social context for *koinōnia* relationships in the context of the Jerusalem collection in "The Jerusalem Collection as Κοινωνία."

32. Longenecker, *Remember the Poor,* 2–6. Examples of this perspective include Hoppe, *There Shall Be No Poor among You;* and Dahl, *Studies in Paul,* 24–25.

33. Longenecker, *Remember the Poor,* 13. Longenecker's book received criticism for its lack of attention to issues of class, or at least social relations, in the Pauline corpus. See Welborn, review of *Remember the Poor.* There

is significant debate about whether class is a useful analysis for biblical studies, especially Pauline studies. See Keddie, Flexsenhar, and Friesen, *Struggle over Class.*

34. Rieger and Kwok, *Occupy Religion.* The promise and pitfalls of Paul for thinking about economic inequality have also occupied recent treatments of Paul in philosophy, particularly Continental philosophy. Reading Romans 7, Ward Blanton writes, "In Paul's confounding of the efficacy of nomos by way of the chance opportunity of this economy's inversion we have a witness to that 'capita' which funded both the promise and the debts of ancient religiosity, the surplus value or excessive forcefulness of its stability and its openness to radical transformation." W. Blanton, *Materialism for the Masses,* 175.

35. Other scholars have drawn our attention toward "the people beside Paul," often with a focus on those on the margins (or marginalized by Paul) in those communities. Joseph Marchal, in a call for focusing on the sexual "bottoms" as a way to reorient our attention in the letters of Paul, writes, "To look to the bottom means rethinking our relations as users *and* recipients. It also entails feeling our way toward being recipients not of Paul's letters but of *their* letters—the ancient recipients of these epistles, named and unnamed, addressed or marginalized, anticipated or unanticipated. We are reading and hearing and passing along *their* mail." Marchal, "Bottoming Out," 232. It is also important to give attention to those who are at the bottom of the socioeconomic ladder and thus are also more likely to be vulnerable in other ways.

36. Philippians is important to this broader conversation because Philippians 4:10–20, whether or not it represents a separate letter fragment, is often characterized as a formal "receipt" for support received by Paul from the Philippian assembly. For further discussion, see the discussion of Philippians 4 in chapter 2. Notably, Philippians 4:10–20 does not include any form of *charis.*

37. These ideas are developed further in Quigley, review of *A Spiritual Economy.*

38. Harrison, *Paul's Language of Grace,* 2, 343. Joubert has explored the Jerusalem collection as an attempt to be a benefactor to that community in *Paul as Benefactor.*

39. Barclay, *Paul and the Gift,* 4.

40. Barclay, 109–30.

41. Harrison, *Paul's Language of Grace,* 656.

42. T. Blanton, *Spiritual Economy.* Blanton also engages with James Carrier ("Emerging Alienation in Production," *Man* 27, no. 3 [1992], "The Gift in Theory and Practice in Melanesia," *Ethnology* 31, no. 2 [1992], and "Gifts, Commodities and Social Relations," *Sociological Forum* 6, no. 1 [1991]), Gretchen Herrmann ("Gift or Commodity?" *American Ethnologist* 24, no. 4 [1997]), and Carole L. Crumley ("A Dialectical Critique of Hier-

archy," in *Power Relations and State Formation*, ed. Thomas C. Patterson and Christine W. Gailey, 155–69 [Washington, DC: American Anthropological Association, 1987], and "Hetarchy and the Analysis of Complex Societies," in *Heterarchy and the Analysis of Complex Societies*, ed. Robert M. Ehrenrich, Carole L. Crumley, and Janet E. Levy, 1–5 [Arlington, VA: American Anthropological Association, 1985]).

43. T. Blanton, 5.

44. David Briones could also be counted among these recent additions. Since Briones's recent book engages more directly with texts and topics related to this study, I will address it in chapter 2.

45. The Letter to the Philippians has been an especially fruitful site of feminist scholarship. Feminist readings from scholars such as Elizabeth Castelli, Cynthia Kittredge, and Joseph Marchal have focused on unity and imitation language throughout the letter. See Castelli, *Imitating Paul*; Kittredge, *Community and Authority*; Marchal, *Philippians*; and Marchal, "With Friends like These . . ." Feminist scholarship on Philippians has noticed the ways in which Paul attempts to assert a hierarchical model of imitation for the Philippians. Language in Philippians related to *mimēsis* (imitation) and *phronein* (having a mind-set) are central to these analyses. For more on *phronein* in Philippians, see Holloway, *Philippians*, 176. This project is deeply influenced by these pieces and simply seeks to add another layer of economic analysis. How is power being negotiated in the theo-economic language of Philippians? Is brokering access to the divine another way in which Paul seeks to exert himself over the Philippian assemblies?

46. Religious expertise, including brokering divine access, favor, and healing, is of course not limited to temple personnel but also includes the proliferation and influence of what Heidi Wendt has called "freelance experts." See Wendt, *At the Temple Gates*.

47. Miller, *Corinthian Democracy*.

Chapter One. Theo-Economics in Antiquity

1. Dignas, *Economy of the Sacred*, 13–35.

2. Eleftheratou, *Acropolis Museum Guide*, 278. For an extended treatment of the sacred financial bureaucracies of ancient Athens, with a focus on *tamiai*, or stewards, see Bubelis, *Hallowed Stewards*.

3. Norena, *Imperial Ideals*, 192; *RIC* 4.1, Septimius Severus 24a. This coin features an eagle on the reverse to signify the emperor's flight to the heavens and an imperial portrait of Pertinax on the obverse, with the inscription "CONSECRATIO" above.

4. Dignas, *Economy of the Sacred*, 2–5.

5. Dignas, 99–101.

6. Dignas, 102.

7. Scheidel, Morris, and Saller, *Cambridge Economic History*. A comprehensive summary of recent scholarship and its intersections with Pauline studies can be found in Hollander, "Roman Economy in the Early Empire."

8. Temin, "Market Economy," 169–81; Temin, *Roman Market Economy*; Finley, *Ancient Economy*. Temin's thesis has grown increasingly popular.

9. Scheidel and Friesen, "Size of the Economy"; Scheidel, "Demography."

10. Bodel, "Slave Labour and Roman Society."

11. Bowman and Wilson, *Quantifying the Roman Economy*.

12. North, *Structure and Change*.

13. The Early Christianity and the Ancient Economy section of the 2017 SBL annual meeting focused entirely on NIE and its usefulness for scholars of early Christianity.

14. Greco-Roman associations and their potential usefulness as comparanda for early Christ communities have been a popular topic of study in New Testament and early Christian studies. Thus, their usefulness (or not) to broader Roman economic history using NIE is important to scholars of early Christianity. See Kloppenborg, "New Institutional Economics."

15. Coase, "New Institutional Economics," 72.

16. E.g., the Delian inventories, which offer significant details about temple accounts, including leases and loans (Dignas, *Economy of the Sacred*, 17). Temple land leases were understood by the grammarian Harpocratian in the third century CE to be the primary source of income to support the bulk of costs for sacrifices (Dignas, 97). For more on temple land leases at Mylasa, which has a significant epigraphic record for these transactions, see Dignas, "Leases of Sacred Property." Leases at Mylasa show an average of 4 percent of purchase price as a leasing rate.

17. While income could be produced from the sale of animals for sacrifice, the costs of public sacrificial animals are listed as expenses in the Delian records for the temple to Apollo. Ekroth, "Animal Sacrifice in Antiquity."

18. See Bogaert, *Banques et banquiers*, 279. For more on the administration of temple loans, see Thompson, "Insurance and Banking."

19. An early example of professional inventory and property management for temples comes from the altar of Khairion, found on the Athenian acropolis probably dating from the mid-sixth century BCE (*IG* I³ 590), making it the earliest extant inscribed cultic monument. The altar contains a dedicatory inscription to Athena, noting that the dedication was made while Khairion served as the tamias. Khairion was one of many Athenian *tamiai*, who "were responsible for the extensive inventories of the classical centuries that document the various possessions of Athena and other gods" (Bubelis, *Hallowed Stewards*, 2). Bubelis's book traces the history of "sacred treasurers," "magistrates who possessed a reasonably significant degree of authority over some kind of sacred property or another" (5). The Athenians regularly published lists of offerings received from 434 BCE to about 300 BCE (Dignas, *Economy of the Sacred*, 16).

20. Parker and Obbink, "Aus der Arbeit."
21. SEG 1.344. Translated in Dignas, *Economy of the Sacred*, 21.
22. Bogaert, *Banques et banquiers*, 279–80.
23. Parker and Obbink, "Aus der Arbeit," 237–38.
24. SEG 1.344. Translated in Dignas, *Economy of the Sacred*, 22. See also Parker and Obbink, "Aus der Arbeit," 238. For the squeezes and photos Parker and Obbink use, see Crowther, "Aus der Arbeit."
25. Dignas, *Economy of the Sacred*, 122.
26. *IJO* 1.65.
27. *IJO* 1.69.
28. Vulic, "Inscription greque de Stobi," 291–98.
29. Translation adapted from *IJO* 1.63–64.
30. The use of "sacred funds" here is interesting, as *tōn hagiōn* seems to suggest that the Jewish community maintains its own sacred treasury. This language offers a conceptual parallel to the Roman imperial treasury, which was often referred to as the *ierōtaton tameion*, but it is still unclear what makes money sacred or profane. *IJO* 1.69.
31. *IG* 4.190.
32. *IJO* 1.208.
33. *IJO* 1.208. This formula also used in no. 29 in Kroll, "Greek Inscriptions of the Sardis Synagogue."
34. This is the case for the second temple in Jerusalem. See Mark 11, Luke 19, Matt 21, and John 2. For more, see Hendin, *Guide to Biblical Coins*.
35. Hopkins with Roscoe, "Between Slavery and Freedom."
36. *IJO* 1.170.
37. I am grateful to Tyler Schwaller, whose dissertation research introduced me to thinking about the implications of divine involvement in these slave transactions.
38. Calderini, *La manomissione*; Gibson, *Jewish Manumission Inscriptions*.
39. *IJO* 1.175. It is incredibly difficult, however, to understand the force of Ioudaios's name here and to draw conclusions about his cultic practices beyond this contract at Delphi, especially because of the early date of the inscription in terms of scholarly debates about when and how to translate *ioudaios*. For some recent discussions of this topic, see Yoshiko Reed, "Ioudaios before and after Religion"; and Wills, "Jew, Judean, Judaism in the Ancient Period."
40. *FD 3*, 2.247.
41. Although it is normally my practice to keep the Greek spelling, I follow the Latin spelling of the translation here.
42. Nasrallah, *Archaeology and the Letters of Paul*.
43. De Ruyt, *Macellum*, 329. For more on public markets, see Dickenson, *On the Agora*.
44. De Ruyt, *Macellum*, 373–74. Philippi has a prominent example, explored more later in this chapter.

45. De Ruyt, *Macellum*, 374–76.
46. *CIPh* 2, 132.
47. *CIPh* 2, 117. See also *CIPh* 2, 158, a measuring table dedicated to the Thracian rider found in nearby Kipia.
48. *CIPh* 2, 286. Translation my own.
49. Shell, *Art and Money*, 9.
50. Ephesos was the first city to be called *neokoros*, or temple warden, a term that was used to indicate cities, often in Asia Minor, with an imperial temple granted to them by the Senate and the emperor to be built and managed by that city. Usually one city per province could house a neokorate temple, and Ephesos eventually issued coins and published inscriptions claiming that they were "twice neokorate." See Friesen, *Twice Neokoros*.
51. Price, "Noble Funerals," 57.
52. "Consecratio," accessed 1 April 2019, http://numismatics.org/ocre/results ?q=fulltext%3Aconsecratio&start=260&lang=en; "DV," accessed 1 April 2019, http://numismatics.org/ocre/results?q=fulltext%3ADV&lang=en; "DIV," accessed 1 April 2019, http://numismatics.org/ocre/results?q= fulltext%3ADV&lang=en; "DIVO," accessed 1 April 2019, http://numis matics.org/ocre/results?q=DIVO&lang=en/. Some coins have more than one of these inscription types.
53. *RIC* 1.1650 For more locating this coin and other Philippian issues in the context of early Christ communities in Philippi, see Harrison, "Excavating the Urban and Country Life," 7–11. For more on Philippian coin issues, see Jellonek, "Coins of Philippi."
54. For more on the image and language of Augustus as pontifex maximus and augur, including on coins, see Zanker, *Power of Images*, 126–29.
55. Harrison, "Excavating the Urban and Country Life," 9.
56. Other coins from Philippi regularly depict the centuriation process through Augustus, priests, or other figures at the head of plows. See Harrison, 7–8. For more on centuriation, coinage, and Philippi, see Nasrallah, *Archaeology and the Letters of Paul*, 121.
57. Harvard Art Museums/Arthur M. Sackler Museum, Gift of Walter C. Baker, 1949.82; image copyright Harvard University Art Museums, https:// www.harvardartmuseums.org/collections/object/304018?position=1.
58. *CIPh* 2, 158.
59. The image and invocation of a heroized figure on horseback was widespread in antiquity, including in the area around Philippi. For more on this figure, see Boteva, "'Thracian Horseman' Reconsidered."

Chapter Two. The Venture of the Gospel

1. For a summary of these positions and the parallels between Philippians 1 and 4, see Holloway, *Philippians*, 10–19.
2. Briones, *Paul's Financial Policy*.

3. Briones, 22–24.

4. Briones, 108.

5. Briones, 108.

6. I use this phrase to refer to the variety of terms related to *koinōnia* found in the Letter to the Philippians.

7. There has been an increasing interest in the role of gift exchange in the letters of Paul, and Seneca has been a popular author used for comparative work with Paul. See T. Blanton, *Spiritual Economy;* Barclay, *Paul and the Gift. Charis* has been an important focus of study in these monographs, including Briones's *Paul's Financial Policy.* While gift exchange is an important theme in Paul, it is not the only mode of financial interaction in antiquity, including divine-human financial interaction. These three sources focus on literary rather than material culture evidence and thus overlook the evidence for some of the range of divine-human financial interactions.

8. Ogereau, *Paul's Koinōnia,* 216.

9. Ogereau, 341. Sampley first makes this argument in his essay "*Societas Christi.*" He expands this argument in *Pauline Partnership in Christ.* For more of Ogereau's engagement with Sampley, see Ogereau, *Paul's Koinōnia,* 311–12.

10. Cf. Kloppenborg, *Christ's Associations.*

11. Ogereau, *Paul's Koinōnia,* 353.

12. Ogereau, 308.

13. David Briones's recent *RBL* review worded this critique much more strongly: "To assume that Paul's theology does not influence his understanding of κοινωνία with his churches in the advancement of the gospel (itself a theological endeavor!) seems highly unlikely. . . . Is it right to assume a one-to-one correspondence between κοινων- terms in documentary evidence and Paul's use of the terms in his letters?" Briones, review of *Paul's Koinōnia.* I think Briones attempts to overcorrect Ogereau; I would argue that κοινωνία discourse in Philippians can be both theological and financial, without tension between the two.

14. Ogereau notes that δαι equals τε here.

15. Ogereau, *Paul's Koinōnia,* 403; P.Mich. 5.354 (TM 12165). This excerpt is from lines 17–24.

16. SEG 30.1608.

17. The "τ[ον λ]ίνον" is actually the genitive singular in the Cypriote dialect.

18. Ogereau, *Paul's Koinōnia,* 175.

19. IKafizin 283, for example, references the flax and seed business as belonging to the οἶκος Ἀνδρόκλου. Ogereau, *Paul's Koinōnia,* 176.

20. Phil 1:5.

21. P.Flor. 3.370 (TM 19386). This excerpt is lines 13–17.

22. Ogereau, *Paul's Koinōnia,* 463. Ogereau's translation, with some adjustment. While it is well beyond the scope of this project, I find the frequent

deployment of *kyria* language in sales, lease agreements, and other contracts in order to make a text authoritative and binding fascinating and perhaps worth pursuing as another potential avenue into a feminist rhetorical analysis of this and other texts.

23. Ogereau, 463.

24. Mark A. Jennings has also recently noted the centrality of *koinōnia* as an organizing principle in the letter, arguing that "Paul does not exhort the Philippians to be partners in the advance of the gospel as generally conceived, but rather, that they be his partners in his gospel mission." Jennings, *Price of Partnership*, 25. However, Jennings does not engage with Julian Ogereau's work or fully address the theological and financial implications of a *koinōnia* in the gospel, writing, "*Koinōnia* should not be restricted to financial arrangements" (32).

25. In a recent article, Julien Ogereau compared Phil 4:15 to three papyri and offers the preceding translation for δόσεως καὶ λήμψεως. Ogereau, "Jerusalem Collection as Κοινωνία."

26. My interest in the divine-human theo-economics of Philippians does not rely solely on a reading of the letter as a unity or a compilation of several fragments. In this project, I follow the majority of scholars who currently treat the letter as a unity; however, if Philippians 4 is, as some have argued, a later letter, then it is possible that Paul writes to the Philippian community using *koinōnia* discourse over and against Philippians' self-understanding of their community as an *ekklēsia*. Phil 4:15, then, would represent Paul echoing back their own self-descriptors while continuing to assert *koinōnia* discourse as the dominant model.

27. Miller, *Corinthian Democracy*, 1–2.

28. For a recent discussion, see Flexsenhar, "Echoes in the *Praetorium*." It is also possible to read *praitōrion* as referring to the imperial guard in Rome. See Holloway, *Philippians*, 87.

29. Dodd, *New Testament Studies*, 83.

30. Koester, *History and Literature of Early Christianity*, 131.

31. Gunther, *Paul*, 91.

32. Wansink, *Chained in Christ*, 17.

33. Standhartinger, "Letter from Prison as Hidden Transcript," 109. Among other arguments, Standhartinger notes that "the form of free house arrest, *libera custodia*, implied by Acts was a privilege of the Roman senatorial class and the very highest ranking provincial elites. Paul's case is scarcely comparable to that of the Jewish prince Agrippa or of Locusta, Nero's medical adviser" (110).

34. For example, a cistern in Philippi was honored in later Byzantine times as a prison that held Paul, but there is no evidence that can demonstrate it was a first-century CE prison. Dassmann, "Archaeological Traces of Early Christian Veneration of Paul," 288–92. A building in the Athenian agora that has been identified as a possible prison could also have been

any number of public functional buildings, including a hostel (Wansink, *Chained in Christ*, 39).

35. For an extensive treatment of the relationship between penal strategies and penal practices in the late Roman world, see Hillner, *Prison, Punishment, and Penance*.

36. References to the darkness of prisons are varied, including Philostratus's *Vita Apollonii* 7.31, Cicero's *Verres* 2.5.61, and the *Martyrdom of Perpetua and Felicitas* 3, to take a few better-known examples (Wansink, *Chained in Christ*, 33–34).

37. Philo (*Ebr.* 101) and Diodorus Siculus (31.9.2) both make reference to the stench of enclosed bodies and rotting food and the poor air quality in prisons (Wansink, *Chained in Christ*, 35–36).

38. Lucian's *Tocharis* 29 describes the shocking conditions that Demetrius, visiting his friend Antiphilus in prison, experiences while trying to locate his friend (Wansink, *Chained in Christ*, 36).

39. Here he follows the example of Loveday Alexander's "Hellenistic Letter-Forms and the Structure of Philippians."

40. Paul deploys a number of passive and indirect constructions in Phil 1:12–20. In Phil 1:12, the subject of the sentence is not Paul but the τὰ κατ' ἐμὲ. In Phil 1:16, Paul is deposited for the defense of the gospel (εἰς ἀπολογίαν τοῦ εὐαγγελίου κεῖμαι), and in 1:19, Paul claims that this will turn out for his deliverance (τοῦτό μοι ἀποβήσεται εἰς σωτηρίαν).

41. P.Mich.Mchl 26, text and translation in Winter, *Life and Letters in the Papyri*, 308.

42. Deissmann, *Bibelstudien*, 103–4; Standhartinger "Letter from Prison," 119.

43. Standhartinger, "Letter from Prison," 119–20.

44. *BGU* 1.87, text and translation in Rowlandson, *Women and Society in Greek and Roman Egypt*, 187, lines 22–33.

45. A search of documentary papyri on the papyri.info database for "bebai*" turns up 1,640 hits (http://papyri.info). Thus, while *bebaiōsis* has no forensic counterpart, it does belong in a broader legal-financial context.

46. P.Col. 8.219, text and translation in Gilliam, "Sale of a Slave."

47. P.Col. 10.284, text and translation in Nielsen, "Application for a Lease." The formulaic nature of the contract helps to reconstruct some of the emphasized portion of text that is a lacuna.

48. To take a single example, Herodotus refers to the gold and silver objects stored in Delphi this way (*Histories* 1.51). See entry for "κεῖμαι" in *LSJ*.

49. For more on the language of slavery in Paul, see Schwaller, "Use of Slaves"; and Marchal, "Usefulness of an Onesimus." For more on the ways in which enslaved persons were understood on a person-object spectrum, see DuBois, *Slaves and Other Objects*.

50. Dignas, *Economy of the Sacred*, 20.

51. *LSJ*: "παρακαταθήκη."

52. Bogaert, *Banques et banquiers*, 331–51.

53. Gordon, "Observations on *Depositum Irregulare*."
54. Buckler and Robinson, *Sardis VII*, 2.
55. Translation in Buckler and Robinson, 2.
56. On the broader interest in Pauline studies and gift-giving in antiquity, see T. Blanton, *Spiritual Economy*; and Barclay, *Paul and the Gift*.
57. One example can be found in the cultic association of the family of Silvanus from 60 CE in Trebula Mutuesca, northeast of Rome. Kloppenborg, *Christ's Associations*, 68–71.
58. Peterman, *Paul's Gift from Philippi*, 159.
59. Marchal, *People beside Paul*, 142.
60. See Shaner, *Enslaved Leadership*; Schwaller, "Use of Slaves"; Roth, "Paul and Slavery."
61. See Nasrallah, *Archaeology and the Letters of Paul*; Marchal, *People beside Paul*.
62. Ogereau, *Paul's Koinōnia*.
63. Ogereau, 270–89. Holloway agrees with Ogereau's reading and sees this phrasing as central to understanding Phil 4:10–20 (*Philippians*, 188).
64. "Angel investors" is a contemporary term used to refer to informal investors who invest in a start-up company in exchange for ownership equity.
65. Nasrallah, *Archaeology and the Letters of Paul*, 125.
66. See Briones, *Paul's Financial Policy*; Ogereau, *Paul's Koinōnia*. For more on this subject, see "Another Poverty in Pauline Studies" in the introduction.
67. T. Blanton, *Spiritual Economy*, 114–15.
68. Nasrallah, *Archaeology and the Letters of Paul*, 126. See also Shaner, *Enslaved Leadership*.
69. Quigley and Nasrallah, "Cost and Abundance."
70. P.Oslo 3.78, text and translation in Sherk, *Roman Empire*, 199–200.
71. I will explore this idea further in chapter 3.

Chapter Three. The Christ Commodity

1. The ideas in this section are further developed in Quigley, "Class-ifying the Gods."
2. I am following the lead of Peter Oakes and Richard Ascough in taking the control of resources as a focus for thinking about economic status. In a recent edited volume, Ascough writes a largely positive response to Oakes's "Economic Situation of the Philippian Christians," 81. However, while Oakes defines economics as the "study of the allocation of scarce resources," Ascough offers an alternative definition of economics: "What makes [a commodity] part of the economic system is the control of its distribution. . . . It is that very control that makes it possible for a commodity to become scarce and thus more valuable on the open market. I would suggest that perhaps a more rhetorically compelling definition of economics . . . is to forefront the aspect of control by those in positions of

power. . . . Economics is the control and allocation of resources." Ascough, "Response," 100.

3. I have chosen to translate the title of this text as *Lives for Sale*, though it is often translated as *Philosophies for Sale*.

4. Devin Singh, exploring the image of Christ as currency in late antique Christianity in authors ranging from Macarius of Egypt to Gregory of Nyssa, makes the claim that "Christ is not merely valuable; Christ is value—the central, critical, determinative value in the economy of salvation. . . . Christ as the coin of God comes to the fore as the crucial means of payment in a redemptive exchange." Singh, *Divine Currency*, 131. While I think that Phil 3:7–11 could be read with the image of Christ as currency, I am choosing commodity here for several reasons. First, I am taking currency, as a medium of exchange, as a more specific part of the genus commodity. To read Christ as currency in Phil 3:7–11 might overcommit to specificity where it is unwarranted; while there are useful potential connections between this passage and the texts Singh considers, those examples are far more explicit in their imagery. Second, commodities, as both useful and valuable objects, allow us to consider Christ as profit while also considering Paul's use of slavery language to describe Christ in Philippians 2. One risk of using "commodity" is its very specific implications for Marx, since commodities have no ability to change but rather reflect social relations in exchange. However, I am not intending to invoke Marx here but rather seeking a term that can encompass the reality of the ancient world, which is both a preindustrialist market and slave economy. For more on whether money should be considered a generic category in Marxist thought, see Derpmann, "Money as a Generic Particular."

5. Although εὑρίσκω is often translated more generally, it is also often deployed in the financial sense I have chosen here, in regard to both persons (Christ) and objects (Christ as commodity). See *LSJ*, "εὑρίσκω." One notable example is found in the LXX in Lev 25:47, in which the passive form is used to describe the acquisition of wealth in discussion of jubilee practices. Given the preponderance of financial terminology in the rest of these verses, and the close pairing with the Christ profit on the other side of the "καὶ" with which it parallels, I think the financial sense best fits here.

6. To do this, I found sources by running two proximity searches, one for "kerd* and theo* or thea*" and one for "zēm* and theo* or thea*" on the Thesaurus Lingua Graecae database. It is important to note that these sources include a vast chronological range, and some key texts come from classical Greek authors, such as Theognis, Euripides, and Hesiod. However, all of these authors have significant afterlives in the Roman period.

7. Bruce, *Philippians*, 113.

8. For a recent summary of objective/subjective genitive translation debates with *pistis*, see Morgan, *Roman Faith and Christian Faith*. For more on Morgan and translating Phil 3:9, see "The Benefits of the Christ Profit" later in this chapter.

9. Bloomquist, *Function of Suffering in Philippians*, 134.

10. Ogereau, *Paul's Koinōnia*, 348. Ogereau only briefly references Phil 3:10 in passing three times (565). Since Phil 3:7–11 does not directly relate to disputes over the exact nature of the financial relationship between Paul and the Philippians, Ogereau leaves it aside. Ogereau's project is reasonably limited to his comprehensive gathering of documentary and epigraphic resources for *koinōn* cognates, explaining in a recent *Novum Testamentum* article, "The relevance of this survey vis-à-vis the NT . . . will require other scholars to exploit and explore further the evidence herein gathered." Ogereau, "Survey of Κοινωνία and Its Cognates," 292.

11. Briones argues for a "brokerage model" in which both Paul and the Philippians share mutually in gifts and act as mediators of their possessions under mutual divine obligation. Briones, *Paul's Financial Policy*.

12. Ogereau notes, reviewing Briones, that Briones "hardly explores philologically the economic *termini technici* Paul deploys in the letter . . . [and] settles for what is effectively a very vague definition of κοινωνία (from a philological and sociohistorical perspective)." Ogereau, review of *Paul's Financial Policy*. I might add that despite an interest in coparticipation in suffering through mutual gift-giving, Briones fails to explore the theological implications of language found in Phil 3, which both commodifies Christ and outlines a *koinōnia*, a venture, in suffering.

13. E.g., Barclay, *Paul and the Gift*; T. Blanton, *Spiritual Economy*.

14. Prott, "Römischer Erlass betreffend die öffentliche Bank von Pergamon," 78–89, cited in Macro, "Imperial Provisions," 170. The inscription as a whole measures 0.3 × 0.16 m with varying widths, with letters of 0.008 m height.

15. Macro, "Imperial Provisions," 169.

16. The term here, *aspratura*, is the only known occurrence of the term. Macro tentatively translates this as "kickbacks" (172).

17. IGR 4.352; IvP II,270; OGIS 484 (lines 29–30). Translation from Melville Jones, *Testimonia Numaria*, 392–93.

18. For more on the difficulty in identifying the opponents given the language Paul uses about them in Phil 3:2–3, see Holloway, *Philippians*, 148–53.

19. See Knox, "Theognis." On the Suda, see Jenkins, "Hellenistic Origins."

20. Theognis 1.11.2, in Gerber, *Greek Elegaic Poetry* (translation my own).

21. For more on this, see Scully, "Echoes of the Theogony," 122–59.

22. Hesiod, *Opera et dies* 320–26.

23. These fragments largely come through a first-century CE text of Dio Chrysostom comparing versions of the same story by several tragedians. Euripides, *Fragments: Oedipus-Chrysippus*, 368–73. Scholars have recently

been exploring the connections between tragedy and New Testament texts, including C. Friesen, "Paulus Tragicus." On the regular use and preference of Euripides in grammatical education, see Cribore, *Gymnastics of the Mind*, 198–99. Lucian also famously describes a Cynic mocking an uneducated person (ἀπαίδευτόν τινα) who is reading from Euripides (*Adversus indoctum* 19).

24. Euripides, *Fragments: Oedipus-Chrysippus*, 396–97. The Loeb notes that the last line could also be translated "when it is possible to make yourself like the gods?"

25. Euripides, *Fragments: Aegeus-Meleager*, 252–53.

26. For more recent work on *eusebeia* in New Testament and early Christian studies, see Hoklotubbe, *Civilized Piety*.

27. Athenaeus, *Deipnosophistae* 8.364d–e.

28. This passage does not directly use "kerd*" and "theo*" or "thea*," but it expresses similar theo-economic logics.

29. Lucian, *De sacrificiis* 2.

30. For more on Epaphroditus's role as *leitourgos*, see Nasrallah, *Archaeology and the Letters of Paul*, 126.

31. Even the sacrificial language is complicated, as Paul describes himself as a drink offering.

32. There is popular ancient tradition about Pythagoras being divine or semi-divine. Fragment 191 of Aristotle's lost treatise on the Pythagoreans depicts Pythagoras as a wonder-worker with a thigh of gold, and Iamblichus, about a century after Lucian, also emphasizes Pythagoras's semidivine status. Huffman, "Pythagoras."

33. Lucian, *Vitarum auctio* 54.

34. Ogereau, *Paul's Koinōnia*, 353.

35. Castelli, *Imitating Paul*; Kittredge, *Community and Authority*; Marchal, *Hierarchy, Unity, and Imitation*; Marchal, "With Friends like These."

36. For more on *phronein* in Philippians, see Holloway, *Philippians*, 176.

37. Marchal, *Hierarchy, Unity, and Imitation*, 30–32.

38. The genre of Phil 2:6–7 as a prose hymn or encomium is very contested, as is the question of whether this text is Pauline or pre-Pauline. For more, see Holloway, *Philippians*, 116–17.

39. For more on the ways in which enslaved persons were understood on the human/object spectrum, see DuBois, *Slaves and Other Objects*.

40. This was probably true of the Philippian Christ communities as well. See Marchal, *People beside Paul*, 141–76.

41. Martin, *Slavery as Salvation*, 130.

42. See Callahan, Horsley, and Smith, "Introduction"; and Schwaller, "Use of Slaves."

43. Shaner, *Enslaved Leadership*.

44. For more on the notion of slavery as social death, see Patterson, *Slavery and Social Death*.

45. Briggs, "Can an Enslaved God Liberate?," 146.
46. For more on this, see Schwaller, "Use of Slaves in Early Christianity"; and Marchal, *People beside Paul*, 141–76.
47. A helpful excursus can be found in Holloway, *Philippians*, 165–68. David Downs notes in his recent book that both the subjective- and objective-genitive positions share the understanding that Christ's *pistis* is demonstrated in his suffering and death on the cross. In contrast, Downs argues that when Paul refers to Christ's *pistis*, he is also referring to the faithfulness of the risen and exalted Christ (*Faithfulness of the Risen Christ*, 3). In his specific examination of Phil. 3:9, Downs assumes that the phrase indicates that "God's righteousness is made known or available through Christ's *pistis*" (the subjective-genitive position), but he questions the long-held assumption that Christ's *pistis* is manifested exclusively in his death (144). This is helpful for opening up a space to think about *pistis* in ways other than just Christ's obedience to suffering and death.
48. Morgan, *Roman Faith and Christian Faith*, 2.
49. Scholars who work on this topic have found Morgan's intervention helpful in breaking the scholarly impasse. John Barclay, despite disagreement with Morgan's reading of Galatians, has acknowledged that she offers a third way out of the *pistis Christou* debate. Barclay, review of *Roman Faith and Christian Faith*. In contrast, Peter Oakes has also used Morgan's book to support a rereading of Galatians using her mutuality argument. Oakes, "Pistis as Relational Way of Life."

Chapter Four. The Down Payment of Righteousness

1. The manuscript tradition of the letter is quite poor. Of the nine surviving Greek manuscripts, all break off after 9.2, launching into Barnabas 5.7 and the rest of the letter of Barnabas. Scholars argue, then, that all come from the same exemplar. The rest of the letter is preserved in Latin manuscripts, in Greek through Eusebius's quotations of chapters 9 and 13, and through some Syriac fragments of chapter 12. See Ehrman, *Apostolic Fathers*, 1.329–30.
2. Pol. *Phil.* 11.1–4, in Ehrman, *Apostolic Fathers*.
3. Ehrman, *Apostolic Fathers*, 1.325–26. David Downs has noted the centrality of polemical concerns within the letter and the ways in which they overlap with financial themes (*Alms*, 225–32).
4. Pol. *Phil.* 3.1, in Ehrman, *Apostolic Fathers*.
5. Nasrallah, *Archaeology and the Letters of Paul*, 138.
6. Pol. *Phil.* 13.2, in Ehrman, *Apostolic Fathers*.
7. Ehrman, *Apostolic Fathers*, 1.328.
8. I am grateful to J. Gregory Given for his work and expertise in helping me better understand the stakes of dating and authenticity with the various Ignatius letter collections. Given, "Ignatius of Antioch."

9. See Brent, who still argues for using Polycarp to connect Ignatius into the early second century ("Enigma of Ignatius of Antioch").

10. In doing so, I am following in the line of recent work by Concannon, "Contestations over Apostolic Memory and Ecclesial Power"; and Nasrallah "Empire and Apocalypse."

11. Pol. *Phil.* 2.1, in Ehrman, *Apostolic Fathers*. I have adapted slightly Ehrman's translation. For this usage of *ekzeō*, see also Luke 11:50 and 2 Kgdms 4:11 LXX (= 2 Sam).

12. Downs, *Alms*, 227.

13. Accountability for blood ("to haima") is also the language found in 2 Kgdms 4:11 LXX (= 2 Sam), when David "rewards" Rechab and Banaa for slaying Jebosthe, the son of Saul, by holding them accountable for the blood of an innocent man. It is also found in Luke 11:50, when Jesus criticizes lawyers for serving as witnesses to the death of the prophets; Jesus warns that this generation will be charged with the "blood of all the prophets shed since the foundation of the world, from the blood of Abel to the blood of Zechariah, who perished between the altar and the sanctuary. Yes, I tell you, it will be charged against this generation" (ἵνα ἐκζητηθῇ τὸ αἷμα πάντων τῶν προφητῶν τὸ ἐκκεχυμένον ἀπὸ καταβολῆς κόσμου ἀπὸ τῆς γενεᾶς ταύτης, ἀπὸ αἵματος Ἄβελ ἕως αἵματος Ζαχαρίου τοῦ ἀπολομένου μεταξὺ τοῦ θυσιαστηρίου καὶ τοῦ οἴκου· ναί, λέγω ὑμῖν, ἐκζητηθήσεται ἀπὸ τῆς γενεᾶς ταύτης).

14. See Anderson, *Sin*, 27–39.

15. Col 2:14. For a discussion of this, see Anderson, *Sin*, 113–14.

16. E.g., Jacob of Serug; see Anderson, 126–29.

17. Pol. *Phil.* 8.1, in Ehrman, *Apostolic Fathers*.

18. By "commodity," I simply mean a good that can be bought, sold, or traded. Down payments, as we will see later in this chapter, can come in the form of goods and also cash payment.

19. There are three occurrences of *arrabōn* in the LXX, all in Genesis 38, where it is usually translated as "pledge." However, the Greek words ἐνέχυρον or ἐνεχυράζω are much more frequently used in the LXX to refer to a pledge or vow. The use of *arrabōn* in Genesis 38 appears to be a direct rendering of the Hebrew loan word found in the MT, where "an ἀρραβών is a pledge of security given against future redemption." Wevers, *Notes on the Greek Text of Genesis*, 640. An Aramaic form of *arrabōn* occurs in some of the papyri found in the Cave of Letters near the Dead Sea and dating to the first century CE; there the Aramaic word *ayin-resh-bet* is usually translated as "guarantor." This term derives from the verbal root *'-r-b*, meaning "to enter, come in" and thus "to stand in"; it was widely used in the West Semitic languages, including biblical Hebrew in Genesis 38, where it means "pledge" or "security"; Yadin et al., *Documents from the Bar Kokhba Period*, 188. Kerr notes in his examination of the use of *arrabōn* in Greek law that although the *arrabōn* was not technically part of

the price, in contracts of sale, it functions like a first installment payment. In Roman law, the *arra* was a small amount of money or an article of a different kind that could be given as evidence of contract. Kerr concludes that with regard to an *arrabōn*, "the thing given is related to the thing assured," and thus, in the two passages in the New Testament where *arrabōn* occurs, it should be translated not as "pledge" or "guarantee" but as "first installment" in light of how the metaphor would have functioned in the relationship between God and humans. Kerr, "Arrabōn," 95.

20. Erlemann has noted the commercial use of *arrabōn* in the context of 2 Cor 5:5 ("Der Geist als '*arrabon*'"). See also Oropeza, *Exploring Second Corinthians*, 114. I have not encountered any sources that explore fully the context of the *arrabōn* in Polycarp, especially in its theo-economic context.

21. P.Mich.inv. 249, HGV: *SB* 14,12176, text and translation from Youtie, "Four Short Texts on Papyrus," 286–92. Youtie notes that while the letter could be requesting wine from unripened grapes, it is also possibly referring to oil made from unripe olives; vegetable seed was also sometimes used for oil production.

22. P.Mich.inv. 1972, *SB* 24,16254, text and translation, with some of my own adjustments, from Sijpesteijn, "Labour Contract to Build a Boat," 159–62.

23. The rescript process of petition to the emperor and imperial (or regional on behalf of imperial) response followed strict formulae from the time of Hadrian until Diocletian, and these petition/responses were incredibly common in the administration of the Roman Empire. This inscription predates these formulae. For more on rescripts, see Hauken, *Petition and Response*, i. These petition and response formulae include several literary conventions also found in other correspondence, such as the inscriptio, exordium, narratio, and libellus/precesas, as well as common themes, such as making the preces appeal to the imperial divinity, which, Hauken, argues, "enters the sphere of the religious prayer" (275).

24. SEG 29.751.

25. The translation is from Oliver, "Greek Applications," 543–58. Oliver explains, "The epistle to Cos seems then to have been occasioned by a failure of the city (acting for the appellant) to make the deposit of 2,500 denarii with the Roman financial officer of the province of Asia, and the crucial line 8 seems to me to have been misunderstood. The proconsul is not telling the Coans that some cases are tried by the emperor and others by the provincial authorities. The Coans know that well. Rather the proconsul is reminding them that even cases deemed worthy of the emperor's attention must in every province be screened by the governor" (552).

26. "Apart from the mention of Corbulon the epistle brings four important pieces of information, 1) that mandata for proconsuls went back at least to Claudius, probably to Augustus as Dio said, 2) that an appeal to the emperor (though perhaps only by a non-Roman) was connected with the permission of the city, 3) that in the Julio-Claudian period, at least in Asia,

a deposit of 2,500 denarii was expected from such an appellant, and 4) that notice of the appeal was transmitted by the city to the governor. The permission of the city was required, perhaps but not necessarily, because Cos was a free city" (Oliver, 553).

27. "The danger, as he reminds the Coans in line 20, lies in the opportunity to blackmail others who cannot afford to undertake the expenditure of time and money represented by another trial in a possibly distant Roman court. The appellant cannot frighten and disturb the adversary without risk to himself; he must put up, well beforehand, the equivalent of 2,500 denarii, which he will lose if he does not carry through with the appeal" (Oliver, 555).

28. Gaius, *Institutiones* 4.13–14, in "On the Institutes of the Civil Law," 185.

29. Phil 2:16 is cited in Pol. *Phil.* 9.1. Mentioning Ignatius, Zosimus, and especially Paul as exemplars of endurance, Polycarp writes that "they all did not run in vain, but in faith and righteousness" (ὅτι οὗτοι πάντες οὐκ εἰς κενὸν ἔδραμον, ἀλλ᾽ ἐν πίστει καὶ δικαιοσύνη). It is possible, though, that this is instead or additionally a reference to Gal 2:2.

30. Pol. *Phil.* 1.1, in Ehrman, *Apostolic Fathers*. Although Polycarp is aware of the Philippians having received correspondence from Paul, and although Polycarp mentions forwarding letters, I am not trying to suggest that Polycarp or (a) scribe(s) are sitting with multiple copies of Philippians and other texts, copying. See Bagnall, *Everyday Writing*; Haines-Eitzen, *Guardians of Letters*; Johnson, *Readers and Reading Culture*.

31. Cf. Phil 1:7–9, 2:25–26, 3:17–21, 4:10–20. For another example of an early Christian making similar arguments, see Dionysios of Corinth, discussed in Concannon, *Assembling Early Christianity*.

32. Pol. *Phil.* 8.2: μιμηταὶ οὖν γενώμεθα τῆς ὑπομονῆς αὐτοῦ.

33. Pol. *Phil.* 1.2, in Ehrman, *Apostolic Fathers*.

34. Pol. *Phil.* 3.2, in Ehrman, *Apostolic Fathers*.

35. Pol. *Phil.* 3.3, in Ehrman.

36. Pol. *Phil.* 4.1, in Ehrman.

37. Pol. *Phil.* 7.2, in Ehrman.

38. Pol. *Phil.* 7.2, in Ehrman.

39. Pol. *Phil.* 4.3, 5.2, 6.1, in Ehrman.

40. Pol. *Phil.* 10.2, citing Tob 4:10, in Ehrman. The past few years have seen a number of studies on this topic, including Anderson, *Charity*; Brown, *Ransom of the Soul*; Downs, *Alms*; Gray, "Redemptive Almsgiving."

41. Pol. *Phil.* 11.1, in Ehrman, *Apostolic Fathers*.

42. Pol. *Phil.* 11.2, in Ehrman.

43. Pol. *Phil.* 11.2, in Ehrman.

44. Pol. *Phil.* 11.3, in Ehrman.

45. Pol. *Phil.* 6.2, in Ehrman (I have adapted the translation for gender inclusivity).

46. Pol. *Phil.* 5.2, in Ehrman, with adjustments.

47. For more on the theo-economic valences of *pistis*, see the previous chapter's treatment of Morgan, *Roman Faith and Christian Faith*.
48. Pol. *Phil.* 2.1, in Ehrman, *Apostolic Fathers*.
49. Pol. *Phil.* 7.1, in Ehrman.

Conclusion

1. For more on this, see Quigley, "Assembling New Possibilities."
2. 1 Corinthians offers an especially promising site for a theo-economic reading. In fact, there is a theo-economic framework at the outset of the letter: the Corinthians are called into a *koinōnia* with Christ (1:9), and the spiritual gifts that this letter contests are described as divine wealth that enriches the Corinthian assemblies (1:5). 1 Corinthians 1 also uses *bebaiōsis*; the Corinthians are given a witness about Christ as a security that insures that the Corinthian assemblies are not in lack (*usterō*); these terms all occur in both 1 Corinthians 1 and Philippians and offer a way to read the opening of 1 Corinthians, and perhaps the whole letter, in a theo-economic light. A theo-economic reading of 1 Corinthians could also serve to build toward a broader comparative study across the letters of Paul.
3. Madani, "Louisiana Pastor."
4. Levin, "Texas Lt. Governor: Old People Should Volunteer."
5. Hays, *Luke's Wealth Ethics*; Kuecker, "Spirit and the 'Other'"; Metzger, *Consumption and Wealth*; Moxnes, *Economy of the Kingdom*; Phillips, *Reading Issues of Wealth and Poverty*.
6. For more on this subject, see Quigley, "Price of Community."
7. For scholarship on gender and Luke-Acts, see Cobb, *Slavery, Gender, Truth, and Power*; Seim, *Double Message*; Levine, *Feminist Companion*.
8. Parker, "Editor's Introduction," xiii.
9. Agamben, *Kingdom and the Glory*; Brown, *Ransom of the Soul*; Brown, *Through the Eye of a Needle*; Rhee, *Loving the Poor, Saving the Rich*; Singh, *Divine Currency*.
10. Frederick, *Colored Television*; Lofton, *Consuming Religion*.
11. Lofton, *Consuming Religion*, 6–7.
12. *CIPh* 2, 158. For a more detailed description of this object, see chapter 1.
13. The image and invocation of a heroized figure on horseback was widespread in antiquity, including in the area around Philippi. For more on this figure, see Boteva, "'Thracian Horseman' Reconsidered."
14. Discussed in chapter 1.

Appendix

1. This verse has several textual variants, including two that read, "for the glory of God and my approval." $\mathfrak{P}^{46}$.
2. This is a theo-economic term, with connotations of labor for wages.

3. ἁρπαγμὸν has been notoriously difficult for scholars to translate. Katherine Shaner has recently argued that the use of sexualized women's bodies to depict conquered peoples suggests that ἁρπαγμός means "rape and robbery" rather than "something to be exploited or grasped," as most major lexica and biblical translations suggest. All of these senses of the term have an economic component, including robbery (taking something that does not rightfully belong to a person) and exploitation, including sexual exploitation (using one's resources to take advantage of others). Shaner, "Seeing Rape and Robbery." There is significantly more work that could be done in the area of gender and theo-economics, but that is beyond the scope of this project. In either case, the deployment of ἁρπαγμὸν emphasizes that Christ only has and uses the resources that are appropriate for his status.

Bibliography

Aegyptische Urkunden aus den Königlichen Museen zu Berlin, Griechische Urkunden. Vol. 1. Berlin: Weidmannsche Buchhandlung, 1895.

Agamben, Giorgio. *The Kingdom and the Glory: For a Theological Genealogy of Economy and Government.* Stanford, CA: Stanford University Press, 2011.

Alexander, Loveday. "Hellenistic Letter-Forms and the Structure of Philippians." *JSNT* 37 (1989): 87–101.

Anderson, Gary A. *Charity: The Place of the Poor in the Biblical Tradition.* New Haven, CT: Yale University Press, 2013.

———. *Sin: A History.* New Haven, CT: Yale University Press, 2009.

Ascough, Richard S. *Paul's Macedonian Associations: The Social Context of Philippians and 1 Thessalonians.* WUNT 2/161. Tübingen: Mohr Siebeck, 2003.

———. "Response: Broadening the Socioeconomic and Religious Context at Philippi." In *The People beside Paul: The Philippian Assembly and History from Below*, edited by Joseph A. Marchal, 95–106. Atlanta: SBL Press, 2015.

Athenaeus. *The Learned Banqueters.* Edited and translated by S. Douglas Olson. 8 vols. LCL. Cambridge, MA: Harvard University Press, 2007–12.

Atkins, E. M., and Robin Osborne. *Poverty in the Roman World.* Cambridge: Cambridge University Press, 2006.

Bagnall, Roger S. *Everyday Writing in the Graeco-Roman East.* Berkeley: University of California Press, 2011.

Bagnall, Roger S., and Dirk D. Obbink, eds. *Columbia Papyri.* Vol. 10. American Studies in Papyrology 34. Atlanta: American Society of Papyrologists, 1996.

Bagnall, Roger S., T. T. Renner, and Klaas A. Worp, eds. *Columbia Papyri.* Vol. 8. American Studies in Papyrology 28. Atlanta: American Society of Papyrologists, 1990.

Barad, Karen. *Meeting the Universe Halfway: Quantum Physics and the Entanglement of Matter.* Durham, NC: Duke University Press, 2007.

Barclay, John M. G. *Paul and the Gift.* Grand Rapids, MI: Eerdmans, 2015.

———. Review of *Roman Faith and Christian Faith: Pistis and Fides in the Early Roman Empire and Early Churches*, by Teresa Morgan. *JTS* 67 (2016): 752–54.

Barton, Carlin A., and Daniel Boyarin. *Imagine No Religion: How Modern Abstractions Hide Ancient Realities*. New York: Fordham University Press, 2016.

Bennett, Jane. *Vibrant Matter: A Political Ecology of Things*. Durham, NC: Duke University Press, 2010.

Blanton, Thomas R., IV. *A Spiritual Economy: Gift Exchange in the Letters of Paul of Tarsus*. New Haven, CT: Yale University Press, 2017.

Blanton, Thomas R., IV, and Raymond Pickett, eds. *Paul and Economics: A Handbook*. Minneapolis: Fortress, 2017.

Blanton, Ward. *A Materialism for the Masses: Saint Paul and the Philosophy of Undying Life*. New York: Columbia University Press, 2014.

Bloomquist, L. Gregory. *The Function of Suffering in Philippians*. JSNTSup 78. Sheffield, UK: JSOT Press, 1993.

Bodel, John. "Slave Labour and Roman Society." In *The Ancient Mediterranean World*, edited by Keith Bradley and Paul Cartledge, 311–36, vol. 1 of *The Cambridge World History of Slavery*, edited by David Eltis and Stanley L. Engerman. Cambridge: Cambridge University Press, 2011.

Bogaert, Raymond. *Banques et banquiers dans les cités grecques*. Leiden: Sijthoff, 1968.

Boteva, Dilyana. "The 'Thracian Horseman' Reconsidered." In *Early Roman Thrace: New Evidence from Bulgaria*, edited by Ian P. Hayes, 84–105. *JRA* Supplement 82. Portsmouth, RI: Journal of Roman Archaeology, 2011.

Bourguet, Emile, ed. *Fouilles de Delphes*. Vol. 3, *Epigraphie*. Paris: Ecole Française d'Athènes, 1910–32.

Bowler, Kate. *Blessed: A History of the American Prosperity Gospel*. New York: Oxford University Press, 2013.

Bowman, Alan, and Andrew Wilson, eds. *Quantifying the Roman Economy: Methods and Problems*. Oxford Studies on the Roman Economy. Oxford: Oxford University Press, 2009.

Brélaz, Cédric, ed. *Corpus des inscriptions grecques et latines de Philippes*. Vol. 2, *La colonie romaine*; Part 1, *La vie publique de la colonie*. Études épigraphiques 6. Athens: Ecole française d'Athènes, 2014.

Brent, Allen. "The Enigma of Ignatius of Antioch." *JEH* 57 (2006): 429–56.

Briggs, Sheila. "Can an Enslaved God Liberate? Hermeneutical Reflections on Philippians 2:6–11." *Semeia* 47 (1989): 137–53.

Briones, David E. *Paul's Financial Policy: A Socio-Theological Approach*. New York: Bloomsbury T&T Clark, 2013.

———. Review of *Paul's Koinonia with the Philippians: A Socio-Historical Investigation of a Pauline Economic Partnership*, by Julien Ogereau. *RBL* 23 October 2016. http://www.bookreviews.org.

Brown, Peter. *The Ransom of the Soul: Afterlife and Wealth in Early Western Christianity*. Cambridge, MA: Harvard University Press, 2015.

———. *Through the Eye of a Needle: Wealth, the Fall of Rome, and the Making of Christianity in the West, 350–550 AD.* Princeton, NJ: Princeton University Press, 2014.

Bruce, F. F. *Philippians.* NIBCNT 11. 1989. Reprint, Grand Rapids, MI: Baker Books, 2011.

Bubelis, William S. *Hallowed Stewards: Solon and the Sacred Treasurers of Ancient Athens.* Ann Arbor: University of Michigan Press, 2016.

Buckler, W. H., and David M. Robinson. *Sardis VII: Part I, Greek and Latin Inscriptions.* Leyden: American Society for the Excavation of Sardis, 1932.

Calderini, Aristide. *La manomissione e la condizione dei liberti in Grecia.* Milan: U. Hoepli, 1908.

Callahan, Allen Dwight, Richard A. Horsley, and Abraham Smith. "Introduction: The Slavery of New Testament Studies." *Semeia* 83–84 (1998): 1–15.

Castelli, Elizabeth. *Imitating Paul: A Discourse of Power.* Louisville, KY: Westminster John Knox, 1991.

Christian Art Gifts. "Leather Checkbook Cover: I Can Do Everything through Him—Philippians 4:13." Accessed 28 April 2018. http://www.christianartgifts.com/Checkbook-Everything-Turq-Brn-Ph-413.

Coase, Ronald. "The New Institutional Economics." *American Economic Review* 88 no. 2 (May 1998): 72–74.

Cobb, Christy. *Slavery, Gender, Truth, and Power in Luke-Acts and Other Ancient Narratives.* New York: Palgrave Macmillan, 2019

Concannon, Cavan W. *Assembling Early Christianity: Trade, Networks, and the Letters of Dionysios of Corinth.* Cambridge: Cambridge University Press, 2017.

———. "Contestations over Apostolic Memory and Ecclesial Power in the Acts of Timothy." *JECS* 24 (2016): 419–46.

Cribore, Raffaella. *Gymnastics of the Mind: Greek Education in Hellenistic and Roman Egypt.* Princeton, NJ: Princeton University Press, 2001.

Crowther, C. V. "Aus der Arbeit der 'Inscriptiones Graecae,'" 4. Koan Decrees for Foreign Judges." *Chiron* 29 (1998): 251–319.

Cyprian. *The Lapsed: The Unity of the Catholic Church.* Translated and annotated by Maurice Bévenot. ACW 25. New York: Newman, 1957.

———. *Treatises.* Translated and edited by Roy J. Deferrari, with *The Dress of Virgins*, translated by Angela Elizabeth Keenan; *Mortality*, translated by Mary Hannan Mahoney, and *The Good of Patience*, translated by Sister George Edward Conway. New York: Fathers of the Church, 1958.

Dahl, Nils. *Studies in Paul.* Philadelphia: Fortress, 1977.

Dassmann, Ernst. "Archaeological Traces of Early Christian Veneration of Paul." In *Paul and the Legacies of Paul*, edited by W. S. Babcock, 281–306. Dallas: Southern Methodist University Press, 1990.

Deissmann, Adolf. *Bibelstudien.* Marburg: Elwert, 1895.

———. *St. Paul: A Study in Social and Religious History.* Translated by Lionel R. M. Strachan. New York: Hodder and Stoughton, 1912.

Delreal, Jose L. "Occupy Protest Shuts Down Harvard Yard." *Harvard Crimson*, 9 November 2011. http://www.thecrimson.com/article/2011/11/9/occupy-protest-shuts-down-harvard-yard/.

Derpmann, Simon. "Money as a Generic Particular: Marx and Simmel on the Structure of Monetary Denominations." *Review of Political Economy* 30, no. 3 (2018): 484–501.

De Ruyt, Claire. *Macellum: Marché Alimentaire des Romains*. Leuven: L'université catholique de Louvain, 1983.

Dickenson, Christopher P. *On the Agora: The Evolution of a Public Space in Hellenistic and Roman Greece*. Leiden: Brill, 2017.

Dignas, Beate. *Economy of the Sacred in Hellenistic and Roman Asia Minor*. OCM. Oxford: Oxford University Press, 2002.

———. "The Leases of Sacred Property at Mylasa: An Alimentary Scheme for the Gods." *Kernos* 13 (2000): 117–26.

Dodd, C. H. *New Testament Studies*. Manchester: Manchester University Press, 1953.

Downs, David J. *Alms: Charity, Reward, and Atonement*. Waco, TX: Baylor University Press, 2016.

———. *The Faithfulness of the Risen Christ: Pistis and the Exalted Lord in the Pauline Letters*. Waco, TX: Baylor University Press, 2019.

DuBois, Page. *Slaves and Other Objects*. Chicago: University of Chicago Press, 2003.

Ehrman, Bart D., ed. and trans. *The Apostolic Fathers*. 2 vols. LCL. Cambridge, MA: Harvard University Press, 2003.

Eitrem, S., and L. Amundsen, eds. *Papyri Osloenses*. Vol. 3. Oslo: Jacob Dybwad, 1936.

Ekroth, Gunnel. "Animal Sacrifice in Antiquity." In *The Oxford Handbook of Animals in Classical Thought and Life*, edited by Gordon Lindsay Campbell, 324–54. Oxford: Oxford University Press, 2014. doi: 10.1093/oxfordhb/9780199589425.013.020.

Eleftheratou, Stamatia, ed. *Acropolis Museum Guide*. Translated by John Leonard. Athens: Pressious Arvanitidis, 2015.

Erlemann, Kurt. "Der Geist als '*arrabon*' (2 Kor 5,5) im Kontext der paulinischen Eschatologie." *ZNW* 83 (1992): 202–23.

Euripides. *Fragments: Aegeus-Meleager*. Edited and translated by Christopher Collard and Martin J. Cropp. LCL. Cambridge, MA: Harvard University Press, 2008.

———. *Fragments: Oedipus-Chrysippus; Other Fragments*. Edited and translated by Christopher Collard and Martin J. Cropp. LCL. Cambridge, MA: Harvard University Press, 2008.

Finley, Moses I. *The Ancient Economy*. Berkeley: University of California Press, 1999.

Flexsenhar, Michael. "Echoes in the *Praetorium*: People, Place, and Protests in Phil 1:13." In *Philippi from* colonia augusta *to* communitas christiana:

Religion and Society in Transition, edited by Steven J. Friesen, Daniel N. Schowalter, and Michalis Lychounas. Leiden: Brill, forthcoming.

Frederick, Marla. *Colored Television: American Religion Gone Global*. Stanford, CA: Stanford University Press, 2016.

Friesen, Courtney. "Paulus Tragicus: Staging Apostolic Adversity in 1 Corinthians." *JBL* 134 (2015): 813–32.

Friesen, Steven J. "Poverty in Pauline Studies: Beyond the So-Called New Consensus." *JSNT* 26 (2004): 323–61.

———. *Twice Neokoros: Ephesus, Asia, and the Cult of the Flavian Imperial Family*. RGRW 116. Leiden: Brill, 1993.

Friesen, Steven J., Sarah A. James, and Daniel N. Schowalter. "Inequality in Corinth." In *Corinth in Contrast: Studies in Inequality*, edited by Steven J. Friesen, Sarah A. James, and Daniel N. Schowalter, 1–13. NovTSup 155. Leiden: Brill, 2014.

Gaertringen, Friedrich Hiller von, et al., eds. *Inscriptiones Graecae*. 14 vols. Berlin: Reimer; de Gruyter, 1873—present.

Gaius. "On the Institutes of the Civil Law." In *The Civil Law*, vol. 1, edited and translated by S. P. Scott, 81–222. Union, NJ: Lawbook Exchange, 2006.

Gerber, Douglas E., ed. and trans. *Greek Elegiac Poetry: From the Seventh to the Fifth Centuries BC*. LCL. Cambridge, MA: Harvard University Press, 1999.

Gibson, E. Leigh. *The Jewish Manumission Inscriptions of the Bosporus Kingdom*. TSAJ 75. Tübingen: Mohr Siebeck, 1999.

Gilliam, J. F. "The Sale of a Slave through a Greek Diploma." *JJP* 16–17 (1971): 63–70.

Given, J. Gregory. "Ignatius of Antioch and the Historiography of Early Christianity." PhD diss., Harvard University, 2019.

Gordon, William. "Observations on *Depositum Irregulare*." In *Roman Law, Scots Law and Legal History: Selected Essays*, 61–69. Edinburgh: Edinburgh University Press, 2007.

Gray, Alyssa M. "Redemptive Almsgiving and the Rabbis of Late Antiquity." *JSQ* 18 (2011): 144–84.

Gunther, John J. *Paul: Messenger and Exile; A Study in the Chronology of his Life and Letters*. Valley Forge, PA: Judson, 1972.

Haffner, Medard. *Das Florilegium des Orion*. Stuttgart: Franz Steiner Verlag, 2001.

Haines-Eitzen, Kim. *Guardians of Letters: Literacy, Power, and the Transmitters of Early Christian Literature*. New York: Oxford University Press, 2000.

Harrison, James R. "Excavating the Urban and Country Life." In *The First Urban Churches*, vol. 4, *Roman Philippi*, edited by James R. Harrison and L. L. Welborn, 1–62. Atlanta: SBL Press, 2018.

———. *Paul's Language of Grace in Its Greco-Roman Context*. Tübingen: Mohr Siebeck, 2003.

Hauken, Tor. *Petition and Response: An Epigraphic Study of Petitions to Roman Emperors 181–249.* Monographs from the Norwegian Institute at Athens 2. Bergen: Norwegian Institute at Athens, 1998.

Hays, C. M. *Luke's Wealth Ethics: A Study in Their Coherence and Character.* Tübingen: Mohr Siebeck, 2010.

Hendin, David. *Guide to Biblical Coins.* 5th ed. New York: Amphora, 2010.

Hengel, Martin, with Roland Deines. *The Pre-Christian Paul.* London: SCM; Philadelphia: Trinity, 1991.

Hesiod. *Theogony, Works and Days, Testimonia.* Edited and translated by Glenn W. Most. LCL. Cambridge, MA: Harvard University Press, 2006.

Hillner, Julia. *Prison, Punishment, and Penance in Late Antiquity.* Cambridge: Cambridge University Press, 2015.

Hock, Ronald. *The Social Context of Paul's Ministry: Tentmaking and Apostleship.* Eugene, OR: Wipf and Stock, 1980.

Hoklotubbe, T. Christopher. *Civilized Piety: The Rhetoric of* Pietas *in the Pastoral Epistles and the Roman Empire.* Waco, TX: Baylor University Press, 2017.

Hollander, David B. "Roman Economy in the Early Empire: An Overview." In *Paul and Economics: A Handbook,* ed. Thomas R. Blanton IV and Raymond Pickett, 1–22. Minneapolis: Fortress, 2017.

Holloway, Paul A. *Philippians: A Commentary, Hermeneia.* Minneapolis: Fortress, 2017.

Hopkins, Keith, with P. J. Roscoe. "Between Slavery and Freedom: On Freeing Slaves at Delphi." In *Conquerors and Slaves,* 133–71. Cambridge: Cambridge University Press, 1978.

Hoppe, Leslie J. *There Shall Be No Poor among You: Poverty in the Bible.* Nashville, TN: Abingdon, 2004.

Horsley, G. H. R., and John A. L. Lee. "A Preliminary Checklist of Abbreviations of Greek Epigraphic Volumes." *Epigraphica* 56 (1994): 129–69.

Huffman, Carl. "Pythagoras." *The Stanford Encyclopedia of Philosophy,* edited by Edward N. Zalta. Accessed 28 May 2014. https://plato.stanford.edu/entries/pythagoras/.

Husselman, E. M., A. E. R. Boak, and W. F. Edgerton, eds. *Michigan Papyri.* Vol. 5, *Papyri from Tebtunis, Part II.* University of Michigan Studies, Humanistic Series 29. Ann Arbor: University of Michigan Press, 1944.

Jellonek, Szymon. "The Coins of Philippi: An Example of Colonial Coinage." In *Pecunia Omnes Vincit: The Coins as an Evidence of Propaganda, Reorganization and Forgery,* edited by Barbara Zajac, Alicja Jurkiewicz, Paulina Koczwara, and Szymon Jellonek, 51–60. Krakow: Krakow Institute of Archaeology, 2017.

Jenkins, Romilly J. H. "The Hellenistic Origins of Byzantine Literature." *DOP* 17 (1963): 37–52.

Jennings, Mark A. *The Price of Partnership in the Letter to the Philippians.* New York: Bloomsbury T&T Clark, 2018.

Jindo, Job Y. "Metaphor Theory and Biblical Texts." In *The Oxford Encyclopedia of Biblical Interpretation*, vol. 2, edited by Steven L. McKenzie. Oxford: Oxford University Press, 2013. http://www.oxfordreference.com.ezp-prod1 .hul.harvard.edu/view/10.1093/acref:obso/9780199832262.001.0001/ acref-9780199832262-e-70.

Johnson, William A. *Readers and Reading Culture in the High Roman Empire: A Study of Elite Communities*. Classical Culture and Society. New York: Oxford University Press, 2010.

Joubert, Stephen. *Paul as Benefactor: Reciprocity, Strategy, and Theological Reflection in Paul's Collection*. Tübingen: Mohr Siebeck, 2000.

Keddie, G. Anthony, Michael Flexsenhar, and Stephen J. Friesen, eds. *The Struggle over Class: Socioeconomic Interpretation of Ancient Jewish and Christian Texts*. WGRWSup. Atlanta: SBL Press, forthcoming.

Kerr, James Alastair. "Arrabо̄ | n." *Journal of Theological Studies* 39, no. 1 (April 1988): 92–97.

Kittredge, Cynthia. *Community and Authority: The Rhetoric of Obedience in the Pauline Tradition*. Eugene, OR: Wipf and Stock, 2015.

Kloppenborg, John. *Christ's Associations: Connecting and Belonging in the Ancient City*. New Haven, CT: Yale University Press, 2019.

———. "New Institutional Economics, Euergetism, and Associations." Paper presented at the annual meeting of the SBL, Boston, MA, 20 November 2017.

Knox, Bernard M. W. "Theognis." In *The Cambridge History of Classical Literature*, vol. 1, *Greek Literature*, edited by P. E. Easterling and Bernard M. W. Knox, 136–45. Cambridge: Cambridge University Press, 1985.

Koester, Helmut. *History and Literature of Early Christianity*. Philadelphia: Fortress, 1983.

Kroll, John H. "The Greek Inscriptions of the Sardis Synagogue." *HTR* 94 (2001): 5–55.

Kuecker, Aaron J. "The Spirit and the 'Other,' Satan and the 'Self': Economic Ethics as a Consequence of Identity Transformation in Luke-Acts." In *Engaging Economics: New Testament Scenarios and Early Christian Reception*, edited by Bruce W. Longenecker and Kelly D. Liebengood, 81–103. Grand Rapids, MI: Eerdmans, 2009.

Latour, Bruno. *We Have Never Been Modern*. Translated by Catherine Porter. Cambridge, MA: Harvard University Press, 1993.

Levin, Bess. "Texas Lt. Governor: Old People Should Volunteer to Die to Save the Economy." *Vanity Fair*, 24 March 2020. https://www.vanityfair.com/ news/2020/03/dan-patrick-coronavirus-grandparents.

Levine, Amy-Jill, ed. *A Feminist Companion to the Acts of the Apostles*. New York: T&T Clark, 2004.

Liddell, Henry George, Robert Scott, and Henry Stuart Jones, eds. *A Greek-English Lexicon*. 9th ed. with revised supplement. Oxford: Oxford University Press, 1996.

Lofton, Kathryn. *Consuming Religion: Christian Faith and Practice in a Consumer Culture*. Chicago: University of Chicago Press, 2017.

Longenecker, Bruce W. "Exposing the Economic Middle: A Revised Economy Scale for the Study of Early Urban Christianity." *JSNT* 31 (2009): 243–78.

———. *Remember the Poor: Paul, Poverty, and the Greco-Roman World*. Grand Rapids, MI: Eerdmans, 2010.

Lucian. Translated by A. M. Harmon et al. 8 vols. LCL. Cambridge, MA: Harvard University Press, 1913–67.

Macro, A. D. "Imperial Provisions for Pergamum: *OGIS* 484." *GRBS* 17 (1976): 169–79.

Madani, Doha. "Louisiana Pastor, While on House Arrest, Again Defies Coronavirus Order with Church Service." MSN, 26 April 2020. https://www.msn.com/en-us/news/us/louisiana-pastor-while-on-house-arrest-again-defies-coronavirus-order-with-church-service/ar-BB13e76z.

Marchal, Joseph A. "Bottoming Out: Rethinking the Reception of Receptivity." In *Bodies on the Verge: Queering Pauline Epistles*, edited by Joseph A. Marchal, 209–38. Atlanta: SBL Press, 2019.

———. *Hierarchy, Unity, and Imitation: A Feminist Rhetorical Analysis of Power Dynamics in Paul's Letter to the Philippians*. Atlanta: SBL Press, 2006.

———. *The People beside Paul: The Philippian Assembly and History from Below*. Atlanta: SBL Press, 2015.

———. *Philippians: Historical Problems, Hierarchical Visions, Hysterical Anxieties*. Sheffield, UK: Sheffield Phoenix, 2014.

———. "The Usefulness of an Onesimus: The Sexual Use of Slaves and Paul's Letter to Philemon." *Journal of Biblical Literature* 130, no. 4 (2011): 749–70.

———. "With Friends like These . . . : A Feminist Rhetorical Reconsideration of Scholarship and the Letter to the Philippians." *JSNT* 29, no. 1 (2006): 77–106.

Martin, Dale B. *Slavery as Salvation: The Metaphor of Slavery in Pauline Christianity*. New Haven, CT: Yale University Press, 1990.

Mattingly, Harold, et al., eds. *The Roman Imperial Coinage*. 10 vols. London: Spink, 1923–94.

Melville Jones, John R. *Testimonia Numaria: Greek and Latin Texts Concerning Ancient Greek Coinage*. London: Spink and Son, 1993.

Metzger, James A. *Consumption and Wealth in Luke's Travel Narrative*. Leiden: Brill, 2007.

Michael, E. M., ed. *A Critical Edition of Select Michigan Papyri*. Ann Arbor: University of Michigan, 1966.

Miller, Anna. *Corinthian Democracy: Democratic Discourse in 1 Corinthians*. Eugene, OR: Wipf and Stock, 2015.

Min, Seong-Jae. "Occupy Wall Street and Deliberative Decision-Making: Translating Theory to Practice" *Communication, Culture & Critique* 8, no. 1 (2015): 73–89.

Mitford, Terence B., ed. *The Nymphaeum of Kafizin: The Inscribed Pottery*. Kadmos Supplement 2. Berlin: de Gruyter, 1980.

Morgan, Teresa. *Roman Faith and Christian Faith: Pistis and Fides in the Early Roman Empire and Early Churches*. Oxford: Oxford University Press, 2015.

Moxnes, Halvor. *The Economy of the Kingdom: Social Conflict and Economic Relations in Luke's Gospel*. Philadelphia: Fortress, 1988.

Nasrallah, Laura. *Archaeology and the Letters of Paul*. New York: Oxford University Press, 2019.

———. "Empire and Apocalypse in Thessaloniki: Interpreting the Early Christian Rotunda." *JECS* 13, no. 4 (2005): 465–508.

Nestle, Eberhard, Erwin Nestle, Barbara Aland, Kurt Aland, Johannes Karavidopoulos, Carlo M. Martini, and Bruce M. Metzger, eds. *Novum Testamentum Graece*. 28th ed. Stuttgart: Deutsche Bibelgesellschaft, 2012.

Nielsen, Bruce E. "Application for a Lease of Vineyard Irrigation." *ZPE* 106 (1995): 179–88.

Norena, Carlos. *Imperial Ideals in the Roman West: Representation, Circulation, Power*. New York: Cambridge University Press, 2011.

North, Douglass C. *Structure and Change in Economic History*. New York: Norton, 1981.

Noy, David, Alexander Panayotow, and Hanswulf Bloedhorn, eds. *Inscriptiones Judaicae Orientis*. Vol. 1, *Eastern Europe*. TSAJ 101. Tübingen: Mohr Siebeck, 2004.

Oakes, Peter. "The Economic Situation of the Philippian Christians." In *The People beside Paul: The Philippian Assembly and History from Below*, edited by Joseph A. Marchal, 63–82. Atlanta: SBL Press, 2015.

———. "Pistis as Relational Way of Life: An en-Christo-Shaped Solution to the Conundrum of Consistency of Use in Galatians." Paper presented at the annual meeting of the SBL, Boston, MA, 18 November 2018.

Oates, John F., Roger S. Bagnall, Sarah J. Clackson, Alexandra A. O'Brien, Joshua D. Sosin, Terry G. Wilfong, and Klaas A. Worp, eds. *Checklist of Greek, Latin, Demotic and Coptic Papyri, Ostraca and Tablets*. Last updated 1 June 2011. http://scriptorium.lib.duke.edu/papyrus/texts/clist.html.

Ogereau, Julien M. "The Jerusalem Collection as Κοινωνία: Paul's Global Politics of Socio-Economic Equality and Solidarity." *NTS* 58 (2012): 360–78.

———. *Paul's Koinonia with the Philippians*. WUNT 2/377. Tübingen: Mohr Siebeck, 2014.

———. Review of *Paul's Financial Policy: A Socio-theological Approach*, by David E. Briones. *RBL*, 18 June 2015. http://www.bookreviews.org/bookdetail.asp?TitleId=9732.

———. "A Survey of Κοινωνία and Its Cognates in Documentary Sources." *NovT* 57 (2015): 275–94.

Oliver, J. H. "Greek Applications for Roman Trials." *AJP* 100 (1979): 543–58.

Oppenheimer, Mark. "'Christian Economics' Meets the Antiunion Movement." *New York Times*, 30 April 2011. http://www.nytimes.com/2011/04/30/us/ 30beliefs.html.

Oropeza, B. J. *Exploring Second Corinthians: Death and Life, Hardship and Rivalry*. Rhetoric of Religious Antiquity 3. Atlanta: SBL Press, 2016.

"P. 7018: Kaufvertrag über zwei Kamele." Berliner Papyrusdatenbank. Accessed 27 April 2018. http://berlpap.smb.museum/Original/P_07018_R_3_001 .jpg.

Parker, Andrew. "Editor's Introduction: Mimesis and the Division of Labor." In *The Philosopher and His Poor*, by Jacques Rancière, ix–xx. Durham, NC: Duke University Press, 2003.

Parker, Robert, and Dirk Obbink. "Aus der Arbeit der 'Inscriptiones Graecae' VII. Sales of Priesthoods on Cos II." *Chiron* 31 (2001): 229–52.

Patterson, Orlando. *Slavery and Social Death: A Comparative Study*. Cambridge, MA: Harvard University Press, 1982.

Peterlin, Davorin. *Paul's Letter to the Philippians in the Light of Disunity in the Church*. Leiden: Brill, 1995.

Peterman, Gerald W. *Paul's Gift from Philippi: Conventions of Gift-Exchange and Christian Giving*. SNTSMS 92. Cambridge: Cambridge University Press, 1997.

Phillips, Thomas E. *Reading Issues of Wealth and Poverty in Luke-Acts*. Lewiston, NY: Edwin Mellen, 2011.

Price, Simon. "From Noble Funerals to Divine Cult: The Consecration of Roman Emperors." In *Rituals of Royalty: Power and Ceremonial in Traditional Societies*, edited by David Cannadine and Simon Price, 56–105. Cambridge: Cambridge University Press, 1987.

Prott, Hans von. "Römischer Erlass betreffend die öffentliche Bank von Pergamon." *MDAI(A)* 27 (1902): 78–89.

Quigley, Jennifer. "Assembling New Possibilities from the Christ Collectives in Philippi." *Political Theology Network*, 6 August 2020.

———. "Class-ifying the Gods: The Christ Commodity in Philippians 3." In *The Struggle over Class: Socioeconomic Analysis of Ancient Jewish and Christian Texts*, Writings from the Graeco Roman World Supplement Series, ed. Steven J. Friesen, G. Anthony Keddie, and Michael Flexsenhar III. Atlanta: SBL Press, forthcoming.

———. "The Price of Community: Deadly Divine Collections in Acts 5:1–11." SBL presentation in a session cosponsored by the Gospel of Luke, Book of Acts, and Economics in the Ancient World sections, November 2020.

———. Review of *A Spiritual Economy: Gift Exchange in the Letters of Paul of Tarsus*, by Thomas R. Blanton, IV. *AJR*, 5 November 2018. http://www .ancientjewreview.com/articles/2018/7/4/boo-note-a-spiritual-economy -gift-exchange-in-the-letters-of-paul-of-tarsus.

Quigley, Jennifer, and Laura Nasrallah. "Cost and Abundance in Roman Philippi: The Letter to the Philippians in its Context." In *Philippi, from colonia augusta to* communitaschristiana: *Religion and Society in Transition*, edited by Steven J. Friesen, Daniel N. Schowalter, and Michalis Lychounas. Leiden: Brill, forthcoming.

Rancière, Jacques. *The Philosopher and His Poor.* Edited and translated by Andrew Parker. Durham, NC: Duke University Press, 2003.

Rhee, Helen. *Loving the Poor, Saving the Rich: Wealth, Poverty, and Early Christian Formation.* Grand Rapids, MI: Baker, 2012.

Rieger, Jorg, and Kwok Pui-Lan. *Occupy Religion: Theology of the Multitude.* Lanham, MD: Rowan and Littlefield, 2012.

Roth, Ulrike. "Paul and Slavery: Economic Perspectives." In *Paul and Economics: A Handbook*, ed. Thomas R. Blanton IV and Raymond Pickett, 155–82. Minneapolis: Fortress, 2017.

Rowlandson, Jane, ed. *Woman and Society in Greek and Roman Egypt: A Sourcebook.* Cambridge: Cambridge University Press, 1998.

Sammelbuch griechischer Urkunden aus Aegypten. Vol. 24. Wiesbaden: Harrassowitz, 2003.

Sampley, J. Paul. *Pauline Partnership in Christ: Christian Community and Commitment in Light of Roman Law.* Philadelphia: Fortress, 1980.

———. "*Societas Christi:* Roman Law and Paul's Conception of Christian Community." In *God's Christ and His People: Studies in Honour of Nils Alstrup Dahl*, edited by Jacob Jervell and Wayne A. Meeks, 158–74. Oslo: Universitetsforlaget, 1977.

Schiedel, Walter. "Demography." In *The Cambridge Economic History of the Greco-Roman World*, ed. Walter Scheidel, Ian Morris, and Richard Saller, 38–86. Cambridge: Cambridge University Press, 2007.

Schiedel, Walter, and Steven J. Friesen. "The Size of the Economy and the Distribution of Income in the Roman Empire." *JRS* 99 (2009): 61–91.

Scheidel, Walter, Ian Morris, and Richard Saller, eds., *The Cambridge Economic History of the Greco-Roman World.* Cambridge: Cambridge University Press, 2007.

Schwaller, Tyler. "The Use of Slaves in Early Christianity: Slaves as Subjects of Life and Thought." Th.D. diss., Harvard Divinity School, 2017.

Scully, Stephen. "Echoes of the *Theogony* in the Hellenistic and Roman Periods." In *Hesiod's Theogony: From Near Eastern Creation to Paradise Lost*, 122–59. Oxford: Oxford University Press, 2015.

Seim, Turid Karlsen. *The Double Message: Patterns of Gender in Luke-Acts.* Nashville, TN: Abingdon, 1995.

Shaner, Katherine. *Enslaved Leadership in Early Christianity.* New York: Oxford University Press, 2018.

———. "Seeing Rape and Robbery: ἁρπαγμός and the Philippians Christ Hymn (Phil. 2:5–11)." *BibInt* 25 (2017): 342–63.

Shell, Marc. *Art and Money.* Chicago: University of Chicago Press, 1995.

Sherk, Robert K., ed. *The Roman Empire: Augustus to Hadrian.* Translated Documents of Greece and Rome 6. Cambridge: Cambridge University Press, 1988.

Sijpesteijn, P. J. "A Labour Contract to Build a Boat." *ZPE* 111 (1996): 159–62.

Singh, Devin. *Divine Currency: The Theological Power of Money in the West.* Stanford, CA: Stanford University Press, 2018.

Standhartinger, Angela. "Letter from Prison as Hidden Transcript: What It Tells Us about the People at Philippi." In *The People beside Paul: The Philippian Assembly and History from Below,* edited by Joseph A. Marchal, 107–40. Atlanta: SBL Press, 2015.

Still, Todd D. "Did Paul Loathe Manual Labor? Revisiting the Work of Ronald F. Hock on the Apostle's Tentmaking and Social Class." *JBL* 125 (2006): 781–95.

Temin, Peter. "A Market Economy in the Early Roman Empire." *JRS* 91 (2001): 169–81.

———. *The Roman Market Economy.* Princeton, NJ: Princeton University Press, 2013.

Thesaurus Linguae Graecae: A Digital Library of Greek Literature. Accessed 25 April 2018. http://stephanus.tlg.uci.edu/.

The Simple Way. "12 Marks of New Monasticism." Accessed 1 April 2019. http://www.thesimpleway.org/12-marks/.

Thompson, Wesley. "Insurance and Banking." In *Civilization of the Ancient Mediterranean: Greece and Rome,* edited by Michael Grant and Rachel Kitzinger, 831–33. New York: Scribner's Sons, 1988.

Vinogradov, Yurig. "The Greek Colonisation of the Black Sea Region in the Light of Private Lead Letters." In *The Greek Colonisation of the Black Sea Area: Historical Interpretation of Archaeology,* edited by Gocha R. Tsetskhladze, 153–78. Stuttgart: F. Steiner, 1998.

Vitelli, Girolamo, ed. *Papiri greco-egizii: Papiri Fiorentini.* 3 vols. Milan: U. Hoepli, 1906–15.

Vulic, Nikola "Inscription grecque de Stobi." *Bulletin de correspondance hellénique* 56 (1932): 291–98.

Wansink, Craig S. *Chained in Christ: The Experience and Rhetoric of Paul's Imprisonments.* JSNTSup 130. New York: Sheffield Academic, 1996.

Welborn, L. L. Review of *Remember the Poor: Paul, Poverty, and the Greco-Roman World,* by Bruce W. Longenecker. *RBL,* 7 July 2012. http://www.bookreviews.org/bookdetail.asp?TitleID=7899.

Wendt, Heidi. *At the Temple Gates: The Religion of Freelance Experts in the Roman Empire.* New York: Oxford University Press, 2016.

Wevers, John William. *Notes on the Greek Text of Genesis.* Atlanta: Scholars, 1993.

Wilhite, David. "Tertullian on Widows: A North African Appropriation of Pauline Household Economics." In *Engaging Economics: New Testament*

Scenarios and Early Christian Reception, edited by Bruce W. Longenecker and Kelly D. Liebengood, 222–42. Grand Rapids, MI: Eerdmans, 2009.

Wills, Lawrence M. "Jew, Judean, Judaism in the Ancient Period." *Journal of Ancient Judaism* 7, no. 2 (2016): 169–93.

Wilson, John-Paul. "The 'Illiterate Trader'?" *Bulletin of the Institute of Classical Studies* 42 (1997–98): 29–56.

Winter, J. G. *Life and Letters in the Papyri*. Ann Arbor: University of Michigan Press, 1933.

Witherington, Ben, III. *Friendship and Finances in Philippi: The Letter of Paul to the Philippians*. Valley Forge, PA: Trinity, 1994.

Worthen, Molly. "Onward Christian Healthcare?" *New York Times*, 31 January 2015. http://www.nytimes.com/2015/02/01/opinion/sunday/onward-christian-health-care.html?_r=0.

Yadin, Yigael, Jonas C. Greenfield, Ada Yardeni, Baruch A. Levine, eds. *The Documents from the Bar Kokhba Period in the Cave of Letters: Hebrew, Aramaic, and Nabatean-Aramaic Papyri*. Jerusalem: Israel Exploration Society, 2002.

Yoshiko Reed, Annette. "Ioudaios before and after 'Religion.'" *Marginalia Review of Books*, 26 August 2014. http://marginalia.lareviewofbooks.org/ioudaios-religion-annette-yoshiko-reed/.

Youtie, Herbert C. "Four Short Texts on Papyrus." *ZPE* 29 (1978): 286–92.

Zanker, Paul. *The Power of Images in the Age of Augustus*. Translated by Alan Shapiro. Ann Arbor: University of Michigan Press, 1990.

General Index

Index of Ancient Sources